H

GU

DAYS OUT

WITH KIDS

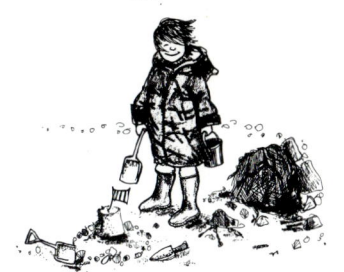

1998/99

NORTH WEST

EDITION

"This book was written in memory of my Grandad, who, along with a dear Nana, would happily squeeze us into the car and set off to explore the delights of the North West".

WITH THANKS TO MY FELLOW RESEARCHERS:
Gregory for his interest, enthusiasm and talent to wriggle behind the scenes. Reuben for his ever ready cafe-sampling abilities. Delilah, who together with Daddy, tried and tested each baby changing room and high chair. And Spencer, more used to following me out of the fire and into the frying pan, who trailed so willingly up hill and down dale.

Thank you

THE HEINZ GUIDE TO DAYS OUT WITH KIDS

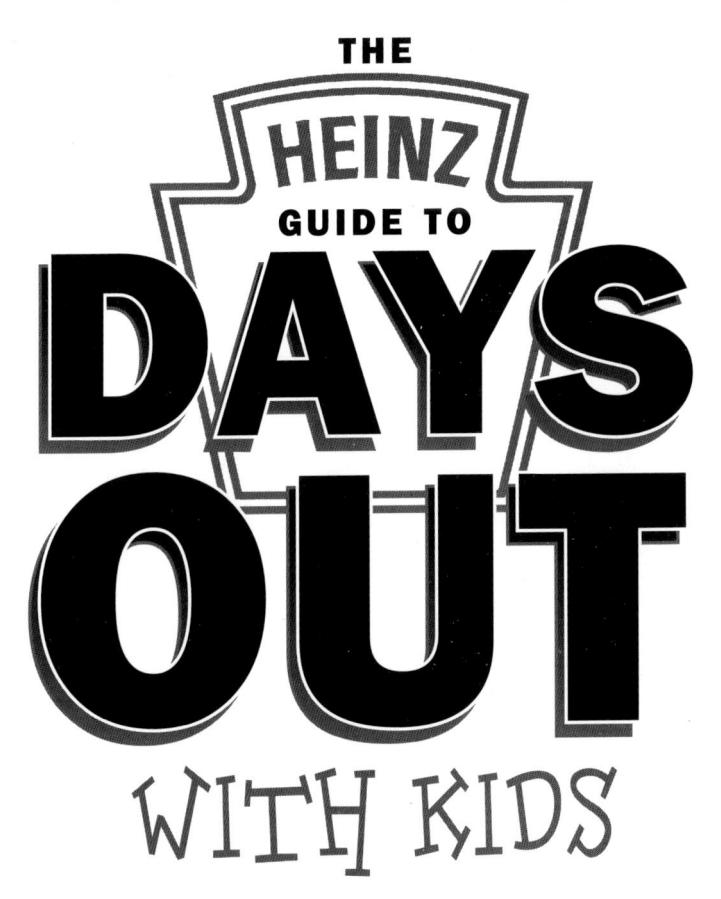

1998/99 EDITION

TRIED-AND-TESTED FUN FAMILY OUTINGS IN THE NORTH WEST

Christina May

BON•BON
PUBLISHING

First published in 1998 by
Bon•Bon Publishing
24 Endlesham Road
London SW12 8JU

Copyright © Christina May 1998
except Llangollen Report © BonBon Publishing 1998

Cover Photographs:
Front cover © 1995 Comstock
Back cover shows Cholmondeley Castle, Malpas, Cheshire © Neil Jinkerson of Jarrold Publishing

The right of Christina May to be identified
as the author of this work has been asserted by her in
accordance with the Copyright, Designs and Patents Act 1988.

A catalogue record for this book is available from the
British Library.

All rights reserved. No part of this publication may be
reproduced, transmitted, or stored in a retrieval system,
in any form or by any means, without permission in
writing from the publishers.

Every effort has been made to ensure the accuracy of
information in this book. Details such as opening times
and prices are subject to change and the authors and
publishers cannot accept liability for any errors or
omissions.

ISBN   1-901411-12-5

Series Editor Janet Bonthron
Design by Caroline Grimshaw
Illustrations by Sam Toft

Printed & bound in Finland by
Werner Söderström Osakeyhtiö

Dear Reader

This is the third edition of the Heinz Guide to Days Out with Kids. It really is now the definitive guide of its type and we are proud to be associated with it. We like to think that Heinz foods play a small part in virtually every family's life, so it's very appropriate that we should be sponsoring a book which can help parents make the most of their time with their families. I gather that the guide is also widely used by teachers to plan school trips too.

I hope you find this new edition a useful source of reference and inspiration.

Yours faithfully

JANE ST CLAIR-MILLER
HJ HEINZ

More about

Henry John Heinz was little more than a kid himself when he established his food business. At the age of 16 he began to bottle dried and grated horseradish from the family garden of his home in Sharpsburg, Pennsylvania.

He packed his product in clear glass bottles so that his customers could see he was selling only horseradish - without bits of turnip or other cheap fillers that other people used. Although he could not have known it at the time, he was starting a venture which was to grow into one of the world's great food enterprises.

In 1886 the British got to sample Heinz products for the first time. Henry Heinz visited London with five cases of products and called on Fortnum and Mason, who promptly bought the lot. The first British factory was established in 1905 in Peckham and a custom-made factory was built at Harlesden in north London in the mid 1920s.

That factory still stands and is an important production centre, but it is dwarfed by the factory built in Kitt Green near Wigan in 1959, Europe's largest food factory. Today there are 360 Heinz products in the UK alone, ranging from well-known favourites like Heinz Baked Beans and Heinz Spaghetti through to all sorts of fun meal time treats like Thomas the Tank Engine pasta shapes, Heinz Baked Beans with Pork Sausages and Heinz Spaghetti Hoops with Hot Dogs.

HENRY J HEINZ

A history of Heinz

1844	Henry John Heinz born, Sharpsburg, Pennsylvania
1869	HJ Heinz Company formed
1886	Heinz Tomato Ketchup sold in Fortnum & Mason
1895	Heinz Baked Beans first sold
1910	Cream of Tomato Soup first sold in the UK
1925	Spaghetti added to the company's range
1938	Heinz Baby Food first sold
1946	Heinz Tomato Ketchup first manufactured in UK
1959	Kitt Green factory opened, Europe's largest food factory
1995	Heinz celebrates 100 years of Heinz Baked Beans
1996	Heinz celebrates 100 years of "57 Varieties"

The magic number "57"

In 1896 Henry Heinz spotted a shoe advertisement which read "21 styles". That set him totting up his own products; 56, 57, 58, 59... There were still a few more, but something made him linger on "57". It seemed a distinctive number, so "57 Varieties" it was. Today the worldwide business markets many hundreds of products under various brand names, but the famous "57 Varieties" trademark has passed into the language.

Contents

Introduction	**5**
How To Use This Book	**7**
Map	**10**
Planning Guide	**12**

Animal Encounters

Bleakholt Animal Sanctuary	**15**
Chester Zoo	**18**
Docker Park Farm	**21**
Knowsley Safari Park	**24**
Stockley Farm	**27**
Windmill Animal Farm	**30**

Look! Look! Look!

Astley Hall	**33**
Blackpool Sea Life Centre & Town	**36**
The British Commercial Vehicle Museum	**39**
Catalyst	**42**
Eureka!	**45**
Leighton Hall	**48**
Martin Mere Wildfowl & Wetland Centre	**51**
National Railway Museum	**54**
Port Sunlight Village	**57**

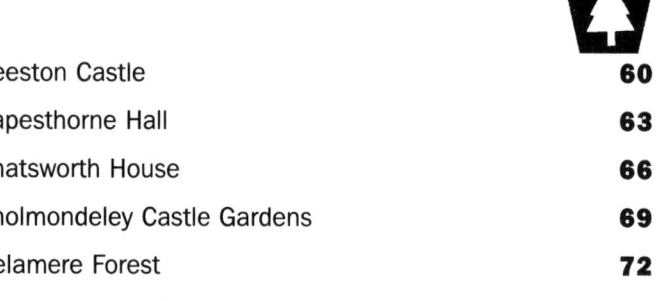

The Great Outdoors

Beeston Castle	**60**
Capesthorne Hall	**63**
Chatsworth House	**66**
Cholmondeley Castle Gardens	**69**
Delamere Forest	**72**
Haigh Hall Park & Craft Centre	**75**
Lever Park	**78**
Tatton Park	**81**

Somewhat Historical

Crewe Railway Age	**84**
Croxteth Hall & Country Park	**87**
Haddon Hall	**90**
Peckforton Castle	**93**
Speke Hall	**96**
Wigan Pier	**99**

Up, Down, There & Back

East Lancashire Railway	**102**
Keighley & Worth Valley Railway	**105**
Llangollen Wharf & Steam Railway	**108**
Mersey Ferries	**111**

The Sun Has Got His Hat On

Freshfield Red Squirrel Reserve	**114**
Lytham St Annes	**117**
Morecambe Bay	**120**
Southport Promenade & Model Railway Village	**123**

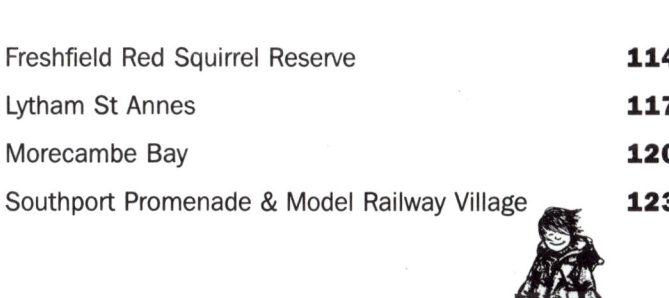

Introduction

WELCOME TO THE HEINZ GUIDE TO DAYS OUT WITH KIDS, WRITTEN for people with children in the North West. Now in its third edition, it is packed with ideas for fun family outings. With lots of trips to try and up-to-date information for 1998/99, I hope that it will help you tackle some of those perennial problems:

WHAT ARE WE GOING TO DO TODAY?
As a mother of three children, I know how important it is to get out of the house some days. Equally, how difficult it can be to think of places to go for a change; places that are not too far; where everyone can have a good time; where young children will be well catered for. This book gives you a personal selection of great outings to choose from; if you go out on one or two a month, there are well over a year's worth of different trips inside!

BUT WHERE IS REALLY GOOD?
Often these days it is not a problem knowing about places to go, but rather whether those places will really be a good trip for people with children. If you've no time to sift through leaflets, or don't know anyone who's been themselves then it can be daunting to try something new. The outings featured in The Heinz Guide to Days Out With Kids have all been done personally, by mothers with children in tow. They are all tried-and-tested recommended trips: we've been there ourselves!

WHAT ABOUT MUMS AND DADS TOO?
If the prospect of yet another adventure playground bores you, then you'll welcome something different. Our aim has been to describe outings enjoyed by everyone in the family, with something to appeal to adults as well as children. Some of the trips may look like just adult outings, but they're not. We want to introduce you to some of the unusual and fun places we have been to. You may all get something different out of the day, but that doesn't matter, as long as you all have a good time.

How Are Places Selected For The Book?

We have included a variety of trips: for the winter and the summer, for rain and sunshine, some nearby, some a greater distance. Some of the trips are old favourites, many times visited. Others were suggested by friends as places that they love. We have noted what childcare facilities are provided in each case: pushchair accessibility, high chairs, nappy tables etc., but haven't selected places purely on this basis. Rather, the facilities information is given on the principle that if you know in advance what is provided you can plan your day accordingly.

All trips were done anonymously. No one has paid to be included in the book, and the views and opinions expressed are very much personal thoughts and reactions. Places are in the book because we had a good time there, and think that other people with children could too.

What Ages Of Children Are Covered?

The book is aimed at people with babies, toddlers and school-aged children. Many of the trips will also appeal to children up to early teens, and, of course, adults too! The facts given for each outing have been checked rigorously. However, things do change, and please check details (particularly opening times) before you set out.

Finally, we'd love to receive your comments on any of the places you visit from this book. Also any of your ideas on places we could include in the next edition. The ten best suggestions we are sent will receive a copy of the new edition absolutely free. Please send them to me at the address below.

Janet Bonthron
Series Editor
Bon•Bon Ventures
24 Endlesham Road
London SW12 8JU

How To Use This Book

EACH SECTION OF THE BOOK COVERS TRIPS WHICH FALL INTO THE same broad category of attraction. Outings are described alphabetically within the section. If you know what sort of outing you want to do, then just look at the section titles, read the section summaries below, and flick through the entries included in that section. Alternatively, the handy planning guide is a rapid, self-explanatory table for identifying the right trip for you.

ANIMAL ENCOUNTERS covers trips to farms, zoos and other birds and beasties type places. Children and animals are a winning combination, and there are plenty of places around the North West which offer it. We have chosen those which we think are distinctive in some way, for example superb handling opportunities for children, wonderful setting, or unusual or imaginatively-displayed animals. Try them all for variety!

LOOK! LOOK! LOOK! features places with exhibitions or displays which children should particularly enjoy, be they of science and discovery (Catalyst), trucks and buses (Leyland Commercial Vehicles) or nose-to-nose contact with deep-sea creatures (Sea Life Centre). These outings offer the chance for children to see something unusual or to experience at close quarters something they may only have seen on television.

THE GREAT OUTDOORS is about trips which are all or mostly outdoors in character, in an especially beautiful or quiet setting. Ideal for walks and strolls, with plenty to see for adults whilst the little horrors run around exhausting themselves. Couldn't be better!

SOMEWHAT HISTORICAL attractions all have a bygone age theme. Your children may not fully appreciate the historical connotations, but will be able to enjoy the setting and exhibits, whilst you can wallow in romantic nostalgia!

UP, DOWN, THERE & BACK has steam train and boat ride outings. Puffs of steam and the smell of smoke in the air are always thrilling and the ones we have included have features which make them particularly accessible. Eat your heart out, Thomas the Tank Engine!

THE SUN HAS GOT HIS HAT ON includes beaches and picnic spots that are our favourite places to go when it's hot and sunny. There is something about spreading your blanket and unpacking boxes and plates of picnic food that is just pure summertime, and you can't beat it. Happy munching! Of course, many of the locations in the previous sections are also excellent picnic spots.

IF YOU DON'T MIND WHAT SORT OF ATTRACTION YOU GO TO, BUT HAVE other criteria (such as the weather, distance, or means of transport for example) which you need to satisfy, then the best way to use the book is to refer to the map and planning guide given on the following pages. These should help you to pick a suitable day out.

THE PLANNING GUIDE can help you select an outing by distance, prevailing weather, admittance to dogs, accessibility by public transport, or opening hours.
* Free, or particularly **good value**, trips are asterisked (less than about £10.00 for a family of four).

Distances are approximate, and taken from Manchester. We have erred on the generous side when deciding on the **wet weather** suitability – if there is somewhere to duck inside during an occasional shower then we say 'yes' under the wet weather trip heading. 'No' means, in our view, it would really be quite a miserable trip if it is raining. For people with **dogs**, 'yes' may mean on a lead only, so always take a lead.

With **public transport** accessibility we have indicated what is available, but you may need to do a short walk too in some cases. 'None' or 'limited' means that it would really be hard work going there without a car.

The planning guide also indicates whether **opening** periods are restricted (i.e. if a place is not open all the year, and/or only on some days of the week). For attractions cited as 'all year' opening, this excludes Christmas Day, Boxing Day and New Year's Day, so check if you want to go these days.

Once you have identified a trip that sounds appealing, refer to the detailed description for further information. Page numbers are given in the Planning Guide. The Fact File which accompanies each entry gives the address and telephone number, travel directions and distances, opening times and prices, and an indication of specific facilities (high chairs, nappy change areas, and eating places). Where appropriate, the Fact File also suggests other nearby attractions.

Map

ANIMAL ENCOUNTERS	PAGE
1 BLEAKHOLT ANIMAL SANCTUARY	15
2 CHESTER ZOO	18
3 DOCKER PARK FARM	21
4 KNOWSLEY SAFARI PARK	24
5 STOCKLEY FARM	27
6 WINDMILL ANIMAL FARM	30

LOOK! LOOK! LOOK!	
7 ASTLEY HALL	33
8 BLACKPOOL SEA LIFE CENTRE & TOWN	36
9 THE BRITISH COMMERCIAL VEHICLE MUSEUM	39
10 CATALYST	42
11 EUREKA!	45
12 LEIGHTON HALL	48
13 MARTIN MERE WILDFOWL & WETLAND CENTRE	51
14 NATIONAL RAILWAY MUSEUM	54
15 PORT SUNLIGHT VILLAGE	57

THE GREAT OUTDOORS	
16 BEESTON CASTLE	60
17 CAPESTHORNE HALL	63
18 CHATSWORTH HOUSE	66
19 CHOLMONDELEY CASTLE GARDENS	69
20 DELAMERE FOREST	72
21 HAIGH HALL PARK & CRAFT CENTRE	75
22 LEVER PARK	78
23 TATTON PARK	81

SOMEWHAT HISTORICAL	PAGE
24 CREWE RAILWAY AGE	84
25 CROXTETH HALL & COUNTRY PARK	87
26 HADDON HALL	90
27 PECKFORTON CASTLE	93
28 SPEKE HALL	96
29 WIGAN PIER	99

UP, DOWN, THERE & BACK	
30 EAST LANCASHIRE RAILWAY	102
31 KEIGHLEY & WORTH VALLEY RAILWAY	105
32 LLANGOLLEN WHARF & STEAM RAILWAY	108
33 MERSEY FERRIES	111

THE SUN HAS GOT HIS HAT ON	
34 FRESHFIELD RED SQUIRREL RESERVE	114
35 LYTHAM ST ANNES	117
36 MORECAMBE BAY	120
37 SOUTHPORT PROMENADE & MODEL RAILWAY VILLAGE	123

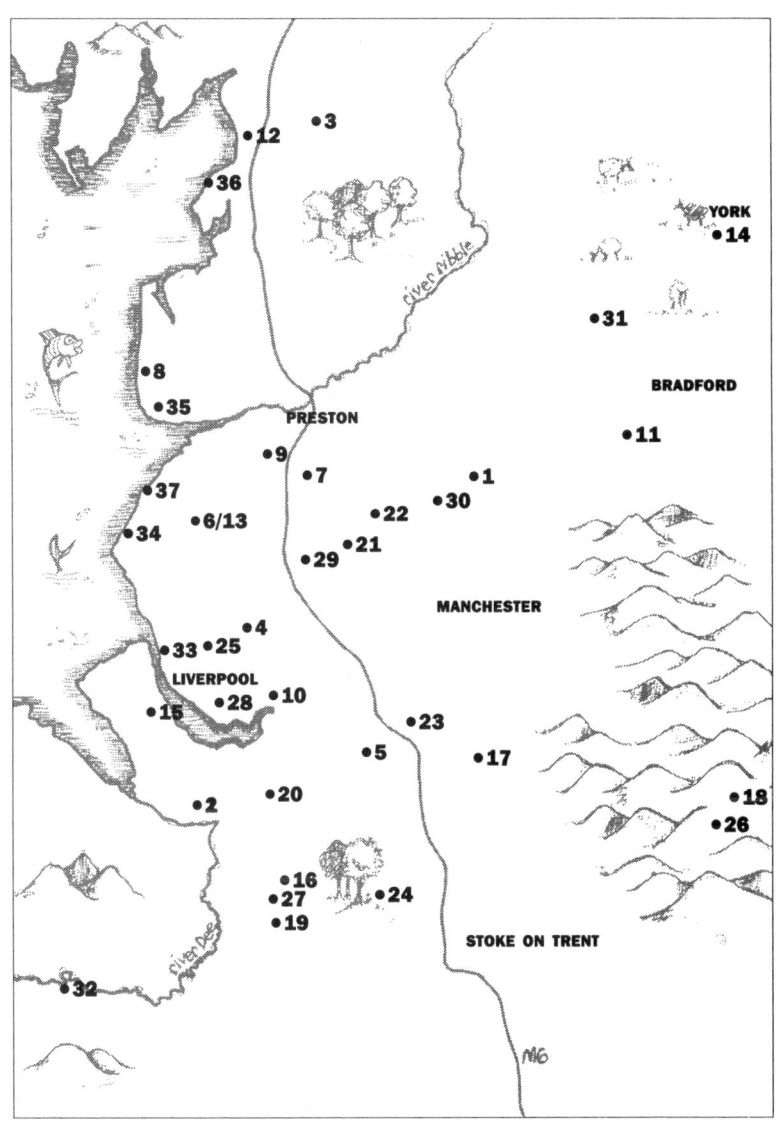

Planning Guide

OUTING	DISTANCE (MILES)	WET WEATHER TRIP	DOGS	PUBLIC TRANSPORT	OPEN	PAGE
ANIMAL ENCOUNTERS						
Bleakholt Animal Sanctuary*	20	NO	YES	NONE	ALL YEAR	15
Chester Zoo	38	YES	NO	TRAIN & BUS	ALL YEAR	18
Docker Park Farm*	60	YES	YES	NONE	RESTRICTED	21
Knowsley Safari Park	30	YES	NO	NONE	RESTRICTED	24
Stockley Farm*	30	YES	YES	NONE	RESTRICTED	27
Windmill Animal Farm*	30	YES	YES	TRAIN & BUS	RESTRICTED	30
LOOK! LOOK! LOOK!						
Astley Hall*	25	YES	NO	BUS	RESTRICTED	33
Blackpool Sea Life Centre And Town	60	YES	NO	TRAIN	ALL YEAR	36
The British Commercial Vehicle Museum	25	YES	NO	TRAIN & BUS	RESTRICTED	39
Catalyst	25	YES	NO	TRAIN	RESTRICTED	42
Eureka!	30	YES	NO	TRAIN	ALL YEAR	45
Leighton Hall	60	YES	NO	NONE	RESTRICTED	48
Martin Mere Wildfowl & Wetland Centre	30	NO	NO	TRAIN	ALL YEAR	51
National Railway Museum	65	YES	NO	TRAIN	ALL YEAR	54
Port Sunlight Village*	45	YES	NO	TRAIN	RESTRICTED	57
THE GREAT OUTDOORS						
Beeston Castle*	50	NO	YES	NONE	ALL YEAR	60
Capesthorne Hall*	20	YES	YES	NONE	RESTRICTED	63
Chatsworth House	50	NO	YES	BUS	RESTRICTED	66
Cholmondeley Castle Gardens*	45	NO	YES	NONE	RESTRICTED	69
Delamere Forest*	35	NO	YES	TRAIN	ALL YEAR	72
Haigh Hall Park & Craft Centre*	25	NO	YES	NONE	ALL YEAR	75
Lever park*	20	NO	YES	BUS	ALL YEAR	78
Tatton Park	15	NO	YES	NONE	RESTRICTED	81

12 HEINZ GUIDE TO DAYS OUT WITH KIDS

OUTING	DISTANCE (MILES)	WET WEATHER TRIP	DOGS	PUBLIC TRANSPORT	OPEN	PAGE
SOMEWHAT HISTORICAL						
Crewe Railway Age*	45	YES	YES	TRAIN	RESTRICTED	84
Croxteth Hall & Country Park*	40	YES	NO	BUS	RESTRICTED	87
Haddon Hall	50	YES	NO	TRAIN & BUS	RESTRICTED	90
Peckforton Castle*	40	YES	NO	NONE	RESTRICTED	93
Speke Hall*	25	YES	NO	BUS	RESTRICTED	96
Wigan Pier	20	YES	NO	TRAIN	RESTRICTED	99
UP, DOWN, THERE & BACK						
East Lancashire Railway	15	YES	YES	TRAIN	RESTRICTED	102
Keighley & Worth Valley Railway	35	YES	YES	TRAIN	RESTRICTED	105
Llangollen Wharf & Steam Railway	60	YES	YES	NONE	RESTRICTED	108
Mersey Ferries*	35	YES	YES	TRAIN	ALL YEAR	111
THE SUN HAS GOT HIS HAT ON						
Freshfield Red Squirrel Reserve*	45	NO	YES	TRAIN	ALL YEAR	114
Lytham St Annes*	60	YES	YES	TRAIN	ALL YEAR	117
Morecambe Bay*	60	YES	YES	TRAIN	ALL YEAR	120
Southport Promenade & Model Railway Village*	40	YES	YES	TRAIN	RESTRICTED	123

SEE **HOW TO USE THIS GUIDE** FOR EXPLANATIONS

Animal Encounters

Bleakholt Animal Sanctuary

And this little piggy had none . . .

BLEAKHOLT IS A FARM OUTING WITH A DIFFERENCE, NOT JUST BECAUSE there is no charge to visit, but because its inhabitants are either retired, sick, or in between new homes. A registered charity, Bleakholt takes in all the waifs, strays and victims of cruelty and neglect from its local Lancashire surroundings.

The farm, typically stone-built and cobbled, sprawls above its surrounding fields, amid green-carpeted hills and tall-chimneyed towns. Numerous outhouses are linked by pathways so you can drop in and take a peek at the clientele in residence. You'll be made to feel welcome just strolling around, making acquaintance with the inhabitants and perhaps hearing from the volunteers what hard luck stories some animals have: a good opportunity to teach children about responsibility and dedication.

"Donkeys, horses and ponies, or even a couple of cows with an interesting tale to tell"

By far the loudest animals are the dogs, and you'll hear them as you arrive. There are several dog pens, heated during the winter, and also a special area for those known, affectionately, as "The Old Woofs". If you've room in your lives for a pet then Bleakholt may be the place to look, although you'll need a home check first and there's also an adoption fee to pay. Our toddler thought the concerto of howls, yaps and bays was great, and danced up and down unconcerned by the fact that many of her entertainers looked like Little Red Riding Hood's adversary. More timid children might not like all this racket, although it is a case of their bark being worse than their bite, the dogs being excited at having visitors, no doubt in the hope that they belong to the volunteer walkies brigade.

Much quieter but more smelly are the catteries. Moggies big and small live in prides in these heated runs, while the older or sick ones are housed in the main building upstairs. There are plenty of them, of various colours. There's even a feral family of pusses, who, not to be left out, have had a hole made for them in the wall of a store room, so that they can bunk up in a covered area, without having their status challenged by domestication.

There's a pond where the rescued water birds can wet their whistles and it is also frequented by sponging, yet equally welcome, wild birds. A picnic bench overlooks it so bring a few extra rolls! Pigeons, hens, and other feathered friends either perch or scratch about in the runs nearby, injured ones returning to the skies as soon as they're well.

Next we came across pigs, two enormous black shapes sounding like a dozing farmhand, huddled together on straw and obviously enjoying a Saturday morning lie in. Once out in the fields you'll find donkeys, horses and ponies. There's even a couple of cows with an interesting tale to tell: one was taken in, aged 17, from a monastery of Tibetan Monks who asked the sanctuary to care for her once her milking days were over. The children were amazed that a cow could live so long and it really made us think, which is probably what a trip out to an animal sanctuary is supposed to do.

There are limited facilities at Bleakholt, a shop, with talking parrot, toilets; a cafe open on Sundays, and picnicing benches. For more substantial fare try the Manor Hotel back towards Rochdale, which has a "Fun Factory".

A few miles down the road is Three Owls Bird Sanctuary, another volunteer-staffed 'last chance saloon'. Call in on the way home (right as you leave Bleakholt and drive through Tern Village). Three Owls is signposted and you could pause at the swings and slides on the village green nearby. The best time to go is on a Sunday afternoon (ring to check first on other days). You'll get a tour of the birds, many of which have party pieces, and have a chin wag with the talking jackdaws. We had quite a lot to talk about, ourselves, all in all, by the time we started off for home!

Fact File

- ADDRESS: Bleakholt Animal Sanctuary, Rochdale Road, Edenfield, Ramsbottom, Lancashire
- TELEPHONE: 01706 822577
- DIRECTIONS: M62, M66, junction 1, right onto A56 to Edenfield Village, A680 towards Rochdale, look out for white sign
- PUBLIC TRANSPORT: None
- DISTANCE: 20 miles
- TRAVEL TIME: 30 minutes
- OPENING: Daily 10.00am-5.00pm (dusk in winter)
- PRICES: Free
- RESTAURANT FACILITIES: Weekends only
- NAPPY CHANGING FACILITIES: No
- HIGH CHAIRS: No
- DOGS: Yes
- PUSHCHAIR-FRIENDLY: Yes
- NEARBY: Three Owls Bird Sanctuary (01706 42162)

Chester Zoo

THIS BIG COLLECTION OF ANIMALS IS SPREAD AROUND AN EXPANSE of landscaped gardens and broad pathways, and with good facilities, picnic areas, and plenty of animal information, you can easily fill a whole day.

We started with the Elephant House, following the signs along a wide path. The Asian elephants were perfectly at one with life and two of them mingled trunks for their doting audience to "aaahh" at. Inside the House, they seemed even larger and when one took a drink it sounded like a toilet with a noisy cistern! Their details are displayed so that you can recognise each one and read its origins and age, but you won't have trouble spotting the baby born at the zoo in December 1997. If you want to perk up your roses you can buy some manure: we saw some being dispensed from a wrinkled grey behind and exclamations of "wow" were uttered as it thudded to the floor.

There are often newborn animals, as part of the zoo's work is conserving endangered species and we were pleased to be greeted by a brown speckled baby tapir at one enclosure. Look out too for the baby giraffe, Blair, born in May 1997.

"You will meet the largest colony of chimpanzees in Europe"

You will meet the largest colony of chimpanzees in Europe. Family life can be seen as mothers tend their clinging babies and older chimps allow themselves to be teased by the larger young ones, until their patience wears thin and they deliver a "you've gone far enough" swipe. There was a big male who seemed to be grumbling, Victor Meldrew-like, about something or other while the chattering remonstrations of a female reminded me of myself. The chimps can be viewed at close quarters through the glass of their house if they're not outdoors.

All the children's favourite animals are here; graceful giraffe, zebra and camels in grassy fields; huge fruit bats

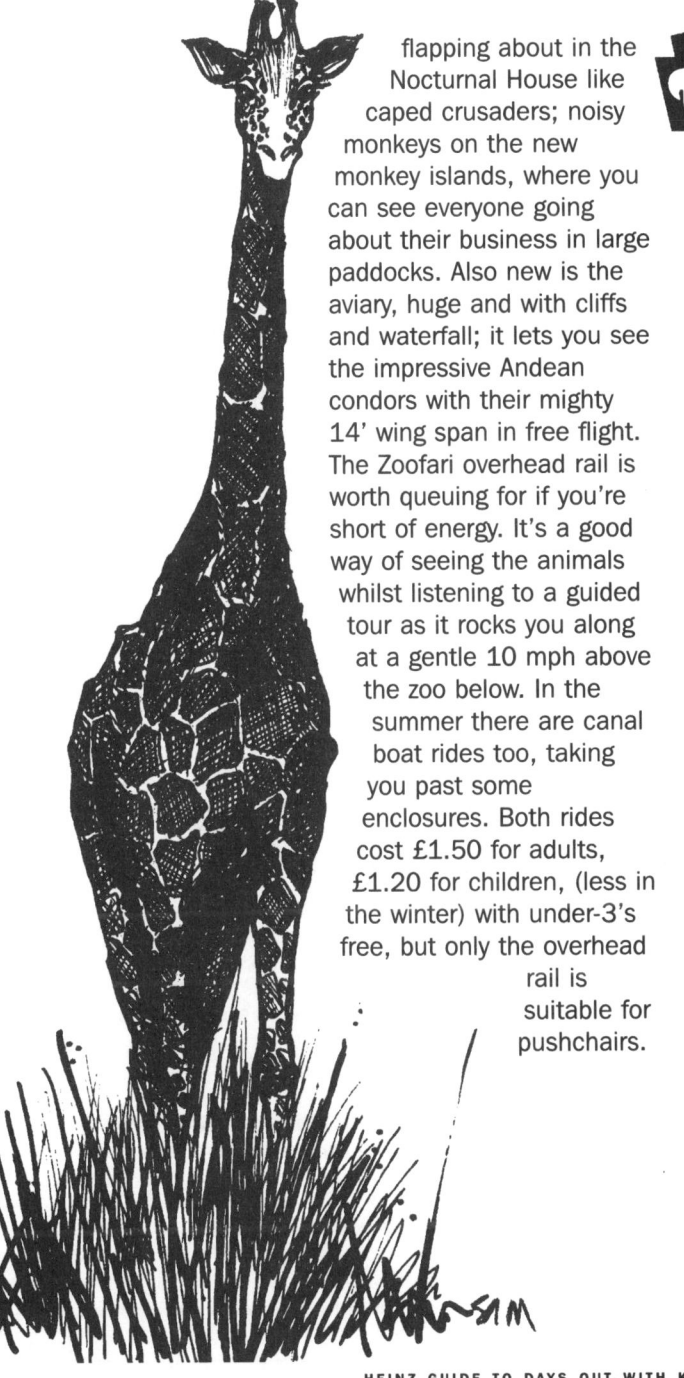

flapping about in the Nocturnal House like caped crusaders; noisy monkeys on the new monkey islands, where you can see everyone going about their business in large paddocks. Also new is the aviary, huge and with cliffs and waterfall; it lets you see the impressive Andean condors with their mighty 14' wing span in free flight. The Zoofari overhead rail is worth queuing for if you're short of energy. It's a good way of seeing the animals whilst listening to a guided tour as it rocks you along at a gentle 10 mph above the zoo below. In the summer there are canal boat rides too, taking you past some enclosures. Both rides cost £1.50 for adults, £1.20 for children, (less in the winter) with under-3's free, but only the overhead rail is suitable for pushchairs.

We clambered from the train and headed for the tiger pen, where we admired one of the world's largest and rarest tigers as he held his head aloft in superiority. There are other big cats in this part of the zoo too, including the now rare Asiatic lions, and four new cubs. Nearby are the penguins: you can watch them underwater through a sunken window, whilst an X-ray of a stricken bird with coins in its stomach aims to persuade visitors not to treat their pool as a wishing well. A small voice piped up that it would be better to spend the money on ice cream and so, after all that looking, we did.

Not far from the restaurant is the children's corner where you can meet less exotic but more cuddly animals. There is also a small play area with swings and slides, and plenty of grassy areas to rest or picnic.

Fact File

- ADDRESS: Chester Zoo, Caughill Road, Upton, Chester, Cheshire
- TELEPHONE: 01244 380280
- DIRECTIONS: M6/M56 to junction 15, then M53 south to junction 12 and follow signs. 2 miles north of Chester on A41
- PUBLIC TRANSPORT: Train to Chester or Bache Station, and bus or 15-minute walk
- DISTANCE: 40 miles
- TRAVEL TIME: 1 hour
- OPENING: Daily 10.00am-5.30pm (summer) or 3.30pm (winter)
- PRICES: Adults £8.50, children £6.00, family £30.00. Under-3's free
- RESTAURANT FACILITIES: Yes
- NAPPY CHANGING FACILITIES: Yes
- HIGH CHAIRS: Yes
- DOGS: No
- PUSHCHAIR-FRIENDLY: Yes
- NEARBY: Chester with its Roman architecture, exclusive shopping and tourist attractions

Docker Park Farm
Eey-aie-eey-aie-oohh!

LIKE A BUTTON SEWN ONTO A PATCHWORK QUILT, DOCKER PARK FARM sits where the hills and fields of Lancashire, Cumbria and Yorkshire meet. It has plenty of friendly animals and opportunities for hands-on encounters, with oodles of fresh country air.

Check the notice board at the entrance giving times of egg collecting, lamb feeding, tractor and pony rides. We arrived just in time for lamb feeding and joined the stampede of buggies and wellingtons that tore over to the pen where a young lass stood with baby bottles, ready to give as many small visitors as possible a turn to be mother.

Near the lambs are pygmy goats whose soprano bleats compete with the trumpeting bellows of beef bulls. These noisy fellows caused our normally placid baby some anxiety although she was soon distracted by a passing crumple-faced pot bellied pig and gave it a prod.

Have a look at the owl sanctuary, where young owls, bred and reared in captivity, wait to be set free into the wild. Nearby, we found the hatchery where fluffy balls of feathers squeaked beneath warm lights. If you're lucky you might catch an egg hatching: in fact you may witness any of the animals being born so be prepared to field questions on the way home!

> **"The morning of our visit a litter of pigs had arrived"**

The morning of our visit a litter of pigs had arrived and we had a good ogle at the sleeping pile of piglets. There were plenty of other small pink blobs in the Piggery with notices giving dates of birth and the resounding grunts and snorts here went into overdrive at feeding time. My eldest was given a bucket of feed to shovel in whilst his little brother watched with his hands over his ears. No wonder these were the beasts used for the sound effects

☞ in the film 'Leon the Pig Farmer'!

Soon it was milking time and we hurried into the shed. There are two dairy cows here to demonstrate this process and a wooden effigy with movable udders stands nearby for have-a-go kids like ours. After much

amusement (and comparison with my feeding the baby), we went outside again and had a go at spotting the hidden animals in the Swan Lake puzzle.

If your rabble have any energy left, head for the straw-filled barn where there is a wooden fort, wobbly board, scramble net and slide for the more adventurous mini farmers, and a smaller area with sit and ride tractors for under-5's. If you've any time left you can have a 70p pony ride (hats provided) or hire a rod for £1.50 and catch a trout from the jetty – taking it home costs another £1.50 but it beats Captain Birdseye fins down!

For 25p we found ourselves sat on a trailer, clutching onto bales of hay behind a speeding tractor bumping around a hilly field with a black calf gambolling alongside. After a few minutes the farmer stopped to give more insights into his farm, before a further bounce across the field returned us to alight by the lambs where we had a final potter about the yard. After a quick browse in the souvenir shop we bid the ponies and heavy horses goodbye and head homewards through the idyllic countryside, back to the city with its dogs, cats, roads and cars, cars, cars.

Fact File

- ADDRESS: Docker Park Farm, Arkholme, near Carnforth, Lancashire
- TELEPHONE: 01524 221331
- DIRECTIONS: M6 junction 35 to Carnforth, and take the B6254 towards Kirkby Lonsdale. Signposted off this road
- PUBLIC TRANSPORT: None
- DISTANCE: 60 miles
- TRAVEL TIME: One hour 30 minutes
- OPENING: Mid February to end October 10.30am-5.00pm. Weekends only until Easter then daily. Open daily during February half term
- PRICES: Adults £3.00, children £2.00, under-2's free. Family £9.00
- RESTAURANT FACILITIES: Yes
- NAPPY CHANGING FACILITIES: Yes
- HIGH CHAIRS: Yes
- DOGS: Yes
- PUSHCHAIR-FRIENDLY: Yes
- NEARBY: Picturesque villages are numerous; follow brown signs for White Scar Caves (no push-chairs) or carry on to Clapham Caves if you're in the mood for a ramble

Knowsley Safari Park

THIS IS A MOST EXCITING PLACE TO VISIT AS YOU CAN GET CLOSE TO some of the world's most dangerous animals while it feels as if you're just driving along a country road. There's also an amazing sea-lion show, Pets Corner and Reptile House.

A herd of deer will be the first to greet you, but you rapidly then encounter a family of tigers. All car windows must be shut! We watched two cubs playing with their mother until another vehicle came along, obliging us to crawl on to a large group of lions basking together, the lionesses prowling vigilantly around. With my hands on the wheel, two kids and a baby in tow, I knew just how my feline sisters felt! A little further on a great big lioness approached our car with a stare in her eyes I hadn't seen since the baby snatched our four-year-old's favourite model train. She had a cub's mouth clamped round her tail but rather than loiter long enough to say "aaaahh" we took the hint and skedaddled. Now in the midst of an unenclosed pride I tootled along whilst words like "mega" and "wicked" echoed from the back seat.

> **"Words like "mega" and "wicked" echoed from the back seat"**

We hadn't bought a guide and it was thrilling not to know what we'd find around each curve in the road although it did mean some of the time that we all had a different opinion of what animal we were looking at. I'm convinced that the big herd of elephants was African and the kids were enthralled when one came right up and waved his trunk over us. Friendly llamas and antelopes surrounded us next, but I was begged to go on to the monkeys. As you pass into their section a sign warns that you enter at your own risk and you are advised to keep moving to avoid getting your vehicle damaged. Try explaining that to the kids! We hadn't been in long before one of the smaller baboons leapt onto the wing mirror and pressed its bottom against my window. Then it jumped onto the roof and proceeded to tear the trim off. As we watched through our glass sun roof, to my dismay a couple of others joined him up there and suddenly we had the most popular car in Merseyside!

Having had enough of ape antics, we made our way to the more refined camels, sedately going about their business. There were huge buffalo which seemed friendly enough although most were taking a siesta and enormous rhinos which the children found curiously like cows in

their grazing behaviour. Things went black and white when we drove by the zebra with their enchanting coats and near a group of ostriches who strutted along most regally.

An area at the end of the Safari journey has been set aside for picnics and when we were there a baby elephant was becoming acquainted with some children. Finally you'll reach the car park where the cafe and amusements are. Rides are extra (80p each) and you need to buy your tickets at a kiosk in advance. There are small roundabouts for little children as well as more adventurous ones for bigger kids.

The sea-lion show is well worth the extra cost (£1.50 adults, £1.20 children) and if you've a pushchair they'll open the fire exit to spare the long steep climb up steps. There's time for the children to gaze at the pool and its inhabitants close-up before you are introduced to three sea-lions. They put on a spectacular show and my eldest was delighted to receive a wet fishy kiss on his face. Rather him than me!

We finished our day with the train ride (70p per person), and a quick look at the souvenir kiosks. These sell mostly animal-themed things, with some at pocket money prices.

Fact File

- ADDRESS: Knowsley Safari Park, Prescot, Merseyside
- TELEPHONE: 0151 430 9009
- DIRECTIONS: M62 to junction 6, get on M57 to next junction (2) and follow the brown signs
- PUBLIC TRANSPORT: You need a car for the Safari
- DISTANCE: 30 miles
- TRAVEL TIME: 30 minutes
- OPENING: Daily 10.00am-4.00pm 1 March to 31 October
- PRICES: £12.00 per car. Sea-lion show, Pets Corner and Reptile House extra. £3.00 parking if not touring animals
- RESTAURANT FACILITIES: Yes
- NAPPY CHANGING FACILITIES: Yes
- HIGH CHAIRS: Yes
- DOGS: No, kennel provided (£2.00)
- PUSHCHAIR-FRIENDLY: Yes
- NEARBY: Pilkington Glass Museum is 2 miles away on St Helens road

Stockley Farm

DID YOU CATCH THE EPISODE OF SOOTY WHERE SWEEP CRASHED A car into some hay? Well, here you can see the very hay loft, and not only does this friendly little place admit furry glove puppets, it also makes people, big and small, very welcome.

Aspiring young farmers can bottle-feed the lambs and goats, shovel grain into the troughs of the cows and pigs, feed the hens and rabbits, and stand on the viewing gallery above the milking machines. The impromptu goings-on down on the farm, such as births, are treated in a matter-of-fact manner, whilst the visitors gape and gawp to their hearts' content. There's a gift shop, tearoom, play area and bouncy barn with access to and from the car park via a lengthy tractor ride. So pair up the wellies, put on your jeans, grab the camera, and oh – don't forget the kids.

The car park is on the estate of Arley Hall and it's here you pay for admittance. The tractor comes at short intervals to deposit bedraggled, straw-speckled visitors and pick up the fresh-faced new arrivals. Seated on bales of hay you'll be treated to a long ride through the farm land, up the driveway to the Yard itself. This is a free service and starts the day off nicely. Once at the farm you'll see pygmy goats gambolling about as farm-yardy noises and smells greet you.

> **"Grunts and squeals of pigs delighted our lot when they went in to help with the feeding"**

There's the shed full of umpteen species of cattle, big, small, black, brown, skewbald, with horns and without, as well as a pen where we found a Highland with her woolly calf. The milking cows graze in surrounding fields until late afternoon, when they enter the high-tech computerised milking parlour below the viewing gallery. We noticed a small wet blob by the feet of one cow, and lo and behold she had just produced a daughter!

☞ Throughout the day we watched the pair's progress as Mum first nuzzled and cleaned her baby and later prodded her into a kneeling position, until she eventually struggled onto all four knobbly legs.

The grunts and squeals of pigs delighted our lot when they went in to help with the feeding. There are the usual farm yard Whites and a growing family of Vietnamese Pot Bellied Pigs, whose founder, Percy was adopted by the farm when he was abandoned at a roadside.

A large undercover area, lined with bales of hay, is used for bottle-feeding lambs and goats. Volunteers are herded into here to sit on the hay before the hungry flock comes in and each child who has a turn as mother is presented with a colour-coded sticker, proclaiming their achievement. If you visit during the sheep shearing, the kids can watch as the overdressed sheep are relieved of their fleeces and treated to a medicinal dip.

The duck pond was created for Stockley's young visitors and a gaggle of fowl can be found doing their

thing here. You can even grab a net and have a dip in. The rabbits on the farm are all for stroking and can be bought. I wondered how many bunnies named Stockley and Arley are hutched in households over the North West.

The grassed playground has wooden equipment on which to climb, swing or slide down. There are picnic benches aplenty (more indoors for wet weather) and both of the sand pits have sit-upon-diggers or spades for landscaping toddlers. During story time a shiny-coated, tall Shire horse craned its neck to join in whilst next to it, a dumpy and shaggy Shetland Pony poked its muzzle through its wire boundary.

The tearoom and shop are at the helm of all this. Ices are served through a hatch and a drinks machine enables mini farmhands to quench thirst without losing too many working minutes. Those with time to stop for lunch will find tasty snacks and mouth watering cakes inside the converted barn.

The farm is great for getting some real country air and, if you don anoraks and boots, you can dodge the rain on an unsettled day by scurrying from barn to barn. When it's time to go it'll be easy to extract the kids with the promise of a tractor ride back to the car park!

Fact File

- ADDRESS: Stockley Farm, Arley, Northwich, Cheshire
- TELEPHONE: 01565 777323
- DIRECTIONS: M6 junction 20, or M56 junction 9. Follow signs to Arley Hall and gardens from motorways
- PUBLIC TRANSPORT: None
- DISTANCE: 25 miles
- TRAVEL TIME: 45 minutes
- OPENING: Wednesdays, weekends and Bank Holidays 11.00am-5.00pm from 5 April to end October. Daily, except Mondays, during August. Last ride to farm at 4.00pm
- PRICES: Adults £3.50, children £2.50, family £10.00, under-3's free
- RESTAURANT FACILITIES: Yes
- NAPPY CHANGING FACILITIES: Yes
- HIGH CHAIRS: Yes
- DOGS: Yes
- PUSHCHAIR-FRIENDLY: Yes
- NEARBY: Dunham Massey Hall (0161 941 1025) for National Trust house, deer park and gardens near Altrincham

Windmill Animal Farm

HERE YOUR YOUNGSTERS CAN WALK, RUN AND JUMP WITH A collection of tame farm animals trotting along behind them, rather like a scene from Heidi. There's also a cafe, gift shop, mini railway, adventure playground, and ball pool.

You'll see a number of small agricultural relics as you enter. Inside is the courtyard where plastic tractors scoot around the picnic tables amongst wandering goats. Animal food is 20p a bag and you'll find that the goats, some of them tiny, come sniffing round pockets and carriers. Our baby was very pleased to be visited so often and managed to stroke a couple of noses.

Big wooden gates help to keep the roaming animals within the farm, whilst letting visitors through to each section. There's the barn where sheep, rabbits, pigs

"For a different view of the animals try a ride on the new mini railway"

and deer live. The rabbits have a spacious 'room' in which a village, complete with police station, church, post office and cafe, has been constructed. The bunnies hop from hutch to hutch no doubt oblivious to the function each is deemed to perform, but the children really enjoyed playing amongst them, determining who was the 'policeman' and who the 'vicar'.

The pigs, all of different shapes, sizes and colour, have a stretch of grass outside their sties. Bales of hay are provided to stand on allowing little people to see over the top of the pens. Ours had a stroke of a pot bellied piglet who was snoozing near the fence and claimed its bristly skin felt like Dad's chin on a Sunday.

Further on you'll see deer, whose antlers our four-year-old described as "all tangled like trees", and in the shadow of the tall windmill are the cows. These are an interesting collection of breeds and the coat of the Highland, soft low of the Jersey and bulk of the Aberdeen Angus provide lots to talk about. For a different view of all the animals try a ride on the mini railway (50p per person), which goes around the farm on about a mile of track and includes 2 stations and a lake.

There are many ponies at Windmill Farm, including a herd of tiny plump and shaggy Shetlands which ambles freely around the adventure playground, together with deer and yet more goats. Our kids loved clambering around the equipment with the animals at their feet. There's a sand pit in one corner where spades and trucks have been provided for a good dig. Whilst her big brave brothers had an adventure round the log constructions, and scrambled on the real tractor, our baby tried out the toddler swings and had a 20p ride on a mechanical horse, which went down very well. New in 1998 is a tractor driving course for toddlers.

There are picnic benches around or if the weather's bad you can eat indoors in the cafe alongside where small windows enable you to keep an eye on the little tikes whilst you have a cup of tea. The gift shop has small kiddie purchases among some craft items and you can even take a couple of cakes home with you. Check anorak pockets for small furry creatures, though!

Fact File

- ADDRESS: The Windmill Animal Farm, Red Cat Lane, Burscough, Lancashire
- TELEPHONE: 01704 892282
- DIRECTIONS: M6 to junction 26, and M58 to junction 4. Head on towards Southport, follow the signs for Martin Mere Wetlands, and once you get to Burscough the windmill looms into view
- PUBLIC TRANSPORT: Bus or taxi from station
- DISTANCE: 30 miles
- TRAVEL TIME: 45 minutes
- OPENING: Easter to September, daily 10.00am-5.00pm. October, November, February and March weekends only 10.00am-4.00pm
- PRICES: Adults £2.50, children £1.70, family £7.50. Under-2's free
- RESTAURANT FACILITIES: Yes
- NAPPY CHANGING FACILITIES: Yes
- HIGH CHAIRS: Yes
- DOGS: Yes
- PUSHCHAIR-FRIENDLY: Yes
- NEARBY: Rufford Hall (01704 821254), the National Trust's 15th century house and gardens

Look! Look! Look!

Astley Hall

Dating from Elizabethan times, Astley Hall is a splendid-looking building, set in its own parkland which has an attractive lake, woodlands, play area and pet's corner. There's a cafe and umpteen delightful picnic spots to choose from, and grassed area for frisbee or ball games. Constructed in the 16th century, the estate was given to the people of Chorley early in the 20th century and is now operated by the local council as a museum and art gallery.

There's a short walk from the car park and we made our way around to the spectacular front of the Hall, where the sight of the shimmering lake competes with the many gleaming windows that adorn the east wing. You come in through the Great Hall, where it is worth picking up leaflets on the quiz trails on offer. One entitled 'Home From Home' invites small visitors to compare the way of life in Astley Hall's heyday with their own. Another trail involves wildlife and encourages little eyes to examine the tapestries and carvings that surround the walls and decorate the furnishings.

> **"The highlight for us was the wonderful dressing-up box with a tall mirror"**

Having had bits added-on and altered through the centuries, the rooms all have their own special tales to tell, a different piece of history in each, with information boards to fill you in. The Cromwell Room is where Oliver is said to have rested after the battle of Preston, while the domed Stucco room, with its hidden space behind the fireplace, hints at the years when Catholicism was severely forbidden. As the hall is also Chorley's museum, there's a memorial room for locals killed during the First World War and a gallery with a series of regularly-changing exhibitions.

We particularly enjoyed the reading room, situated in a multiple-windowed room with great views over the greenery of the park outside. There are books here, travel guides and historical references, with tables and chairs placed thoughtfully to encourage you to linger. Children's books have been included, but the highlight for us was the wonderful dressing-up box with a tall mirror, allowing our eldest son to transform into the most sophisticated of ladies, a long red gown trailing along the floor in his wake, little brother to opt for a sparkly blouse and big floppy hat and their sister to be draped in a scarf. RSC eat your heart out!

By the time we'd finished treading the stately boards, it was time to head outside. The lake is wide and elegantly-landscaped. Stone steps lead down to a platform, handy to stand on for feeding the ducks. You can meander along the bank until it comes to an abrupt end, the wide pathway closing it off suddenly, a surprising drop and dry land appearing on the other side.

Trek round to the left and you'll find the pets corner with a collection of goats, hamsters, bunnies, guinea pigs, budgies and domestic fowl in residence. Just a bit further is the play area, from where we eventually extracted the kids by tempting them with the woods. These are quite extensive and offer plenty of exploring potential, as well as a Nature Trail which takes about 45 minutes.

There is a programme of workshops for children in the school holidays, and other events over the summer. Look out for egg decorating and chalk drawing over Easter, or medieval music and archaeology later in the year!

Fact File

- ADDRESS: Astley Hall, Astley Park, Off Hall Gate, Chorley, Lancashire
- TELEPHONE: 01257 515555
- DIRECTIONS: M6 to junction 28, or M61 to junction 8, follow signs to Astley Hall
- PUBLIC TRANSPORT: Bus or 15-20 minutes walk from Chorley
- DISTANCE: 25 miles
- TRAVEL TIME: 30 minutes
- OPENING: 12.00noon-5.00pm daily except Mondays from April to October. Friday-Sunday only 12.00noon-4.00pm the rest of the year
- PRICES: Adults £2.70, children £1.70, family £6.00. Chorley residents free
- RESTAURANT FACILITIES: Yes
- NAPPY CHANGING FACILITIES: Yes
- HIGH CHAIRS: No
- DOGS: Outside only
- PUSHCHAIR-FRIENDLY: No
- NEARBY: Worden Park and Craft Centre (01772 455908)

Blackpool Sea Life Centre & Town

6, 7, 8, 9, 10, then I let it go again

THE VICTORIANS FOUNDED A GREAT DAY OUT WITH THEIR BATHING huts, tram lines and ornate tower at Blackpool. You can walk the Golden Mile; and call in on one of the three Piers, the Tower, Tussaud's Wax Works, the Sand Castle Swimming Extravaganza, the fair with its record-breaking roller coaster, a replica of Coronation Street, or any of the many arcades, souvenir shops and cafes. All can be found, along with the Sea Life Centre, along the Promenade.

If you'd prefer a more leisurely day jump aboard a tram, bus, pony and trap or donkey (if you're small enough!) Tram and bus stops are at frequent intervals along the road, the ponies and traps wait alongside, and the donkeys can be found along the beach for a jingly-jangly lumber up the sand. Opposite the line of colour and lights, away from the Bingo callers and music, the elegance of the Victorian era lives on in the ornate street lamps, covered seating and iron railings. The beach goes on for ever and once on the sand, wherever you plonk yourself, you can gauge distances by looking back at the Tower. Refreshments, meanwhile, are only ever just across the road.

The Sea Life Centre can't be missed, with giant sea creatures emblazoned across it. Inside you'll meet wet beasties, big and small, passive and fierce. There's a lift for pushchairs and even the youngest of children will love peering up, down and around at the swimming, crawling and sleeping animals. There are buttons to press, video screens to watch and noises to hear, and you can read up on all the fascinating facts whilst the kids stare wide-eyed at the exhibits. There's a good scratch card quiz available which people of all ages can enjoy, but unless you like the game of Sardines, don't wait for it to rain before you visit!

Dramatic decor creates a mysterious atmosphere in which to explore the secrets of the deep. Lighting is used effectively, with the noises of the tide, gulls or fun fair bringing it together perfectly, enabling you to drift off into your own imagined lagoon, the graceful sea creatures and atmospheric music easing the stresses of parenthood.

The new tropical tanks are a sight not to be missed, especially the underwater observatory onto Killer Coral. You can lose yourselves amongst the dangers of the deep here as moray eel, stone fish (the most poisonous fish there is) and other nasties lurk just inches away – thankfully behind glass. Don't let it put you off the Touch Pool though, where my eldest nervously encountered a crab. His younger sibling sidled up, pulled out a starfish

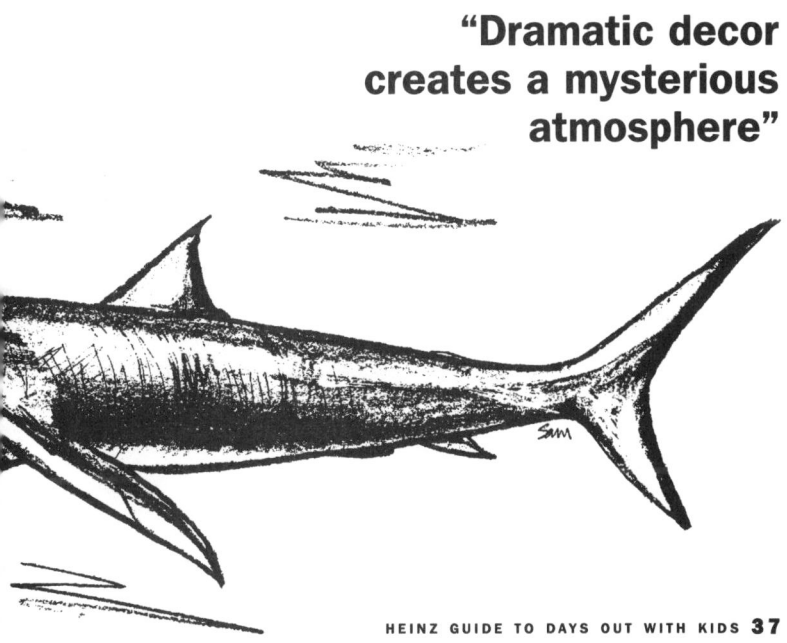

> **"Dramatic decor creates a mysterious atmosphere"**

and proudly popped it into the larger palm of his brother. Eeek! It was back in the pool pretty fast from there.

Have a go at feeling strange things in the touch and guess spot too. Again our 4-year-old had a good poke around whilst his elders recoiled at the thought of having just picked up an octopus's leg: by the time we reached the quay side, it was all we could do to stop him lifting out a sting ray!

We had no such problems with the sharks, however. You enter the Kingdom of the Shark through a passage of rugged rocks and will find yourself closely surrounded by sharks of all shapes and . . . SIZES! Meet them nose to nose through the glass, walk beneath as they glide silently above you, or stand beside the window to see a number of infamous dorsal fins streak past.

Part of the shark tank is visible in the restaurant, which includes fish and chips on the menu! The gift shop is nearby and you go out this way, via a 17th Century timbered street. This includes a moving rat and cries of "Look out below" to illustrate historic sewerage systems (or rather the lack of them). Yorkshire Water – all is forgiven! Walk through the sewer and you're almost out onto the Promenade, where eels are jellied and the sea looks blue.

Fact File

- ADDRESS: Sea Life Centre, Promenade, Blackpool, Lancashire
- TELEPHONE: 01253 622445
- DIRECTIONS: M6 to Preston, junction 32, and M55 on to Blackpool
- PUBLIC TRANSPORT: Train to Blackpool
- DISTANCE: 60 miles
- TRAVEL TIME: 1 hour
- OPENING: Daily from 10.00am. Closing time varies throughout year
- PRICES: £5.95 adults, £4.95 children, under-4's free. Reduced in winter
- RESTAURANT FACILITIES: Yes
- NAPPY CHANGING FACILITIES: Yes
- HIGH CHAIRS: Yes
- DOGS: No
- PUSHCHAIR-FRIENDLY: Yes
- NEARBY: Zoo, Model Village and Stanley Park all signposted and within easy distance

The British Commercial Vehicle Museum

HERE YOU CAN SEE THE LARGEST COLLECTION OF COMMERCIAL vehicles in Europe. For traffic freaks it's a great opportunity to get close to over 50 old vehicles: shiny vans, lorries and buses, and beef up on some of the technical details. Finish off the day at the nearby Worden Park where you'll find a maze, craft centre, miniature railway, crazy golf and playground set within spacious grounds of what was once a stately home.

We pottered around the Leyland museum first. Effective scenery has been painted to give perfect back drops to the exhibits so that the coal van is seen in a cobbled street outside John Grant and Son's grocer's and the ornate Showman's caravan (with delightful furnishings inside) appears to sit within a fairground. This scene is brought to life with an extravagant old fairground organ lending music and lights. The oldest piece in the museum is an 1896 steam van which was declared by the kids to be older than me so it must be pretty ancient!

> **"The highly polished fire engines stationed here look splendid"**

You can see a World War I trench and, with the sound of a crowing cock, the battle commences as planes bomb the town beyond and sharp commands are given to the men with their army vehicles. This re-enactment is repeated every 15 minutes or so. Behind it a painted house emits the noises of someone preparing for bed and it's not long before a fire can be seen smouldering behind a curtain. Things get a bit dramatic but the fire engines are heard to arrive and some brusque instructions ensure the fire is quenched. (I took this as a good opportunity to talk about the dangers of matches!) The highly polished fire engines stationed here look splendid although Fireman Sam enthusiasts can't clamber aboard!

Nearby though, standing in a neat row of vintage buses, is a single decker that is good for a romp and the Pope Mobile (as used by His Holiness during his British tour in 1982) can also be investigated from inside. The Memorabilia shop is well-stocked with model cars, trucks and vans for all those essential presents!

Light refreshments are available inside the Museum. Alternatively, head out to Worden Park where there is a cafe and the tree-dotted open spaces and wooded areas give youngsters a chance to let off their own steam after the confines of the Vehicle Museum. The flat grassed land is well-maintained with neat pathways to ease buggies along and there's an immense playground which has toilets and picnic benches providing an excuse not to move for some time.

We found the crazy golf and had a good game of "how-the-dickens-do-you-get-it-up-there-and-through-that" before crossing a scaled-down iron foot-bridge which passes over a miniature railway offering free rides on Sunday afternoons or bank holidays.

The coffee shop serves home cooked meals and desserts and, being situated within old stables, lends an authentically rustic feel. Also in the cobbled courtyard are the theatre which puts on regular live performances and outbuildings with resident crafts people. Check the notice-board to see who's in or out: you might catch a blacksmith, a wood turner, landscape artist and pyrographer (maker of pictures with a hot poker). This is a good place to buy unusual presents as kids can even boast that they watched them being made!

Fact File

- ADDRESS: British Commercial Vehicle Museum, Kings Street, Leyland, Lancashire
- TELEPHONE: Museum 01772 451011, Worden Park 01772 455908
- DIRECTIONS: Junction 28 off M6, follow the brown signs for both
- PUBLIC TRANSPORT: 10-minute walk from Leyland Station to Museum, 30 minutes to Park. Buses available
- DISTANCE: 25 miles
- TRAVEL TIME: 30 minutes
- OPENING: 10.00am-5.00pm Sundays, Tuesdays, Wednesdays and Bank Holidays from Easter to end September. Sundays only in October. Park daily from daybreak to dusk
- PRICES: Adults £4.00, children £2.00, family £10.00. Park and Craft Centre free
- RESTAURANT FACILITIES: Yes
- NAPPY CHANGING FACILITIES: Yes
- HIGH CHAIRS: No
- DOGS: No
- PUSHCHAIR-FRIENDLY: Yes
- NEARBY: The picturesque Cuerden Valley Park

Catalyst

THIS MINE OF INFORMATION, PERCHED ON THE WEST BANK OF THE Mersey, offers buttons to press and experiments to try. It guides you through the history of the chemical industry, in particular its contributions in the North West, and lets you in on a few secrets.

Two giant caustic soda pots mark the entrance, and as we approached the children got excited by the sight of passengers in the glass elevator that glides up and down the outer wall. By the reception desk the wheels and pistons of a dry vacuum pump work away. Buy a "Family Fun Trail" leaflet (25p), a quiz designed to be tackled by family groups as they work their way round.

Each exhibit has detailed information on its origin and uses within the chemical industry and while smaller visitors enjoy the lights and other visual changes, older ones can take in as much factual information as they wish to. Speaking as someone who scored 10% at my last chemistry exam, a lot of the theory was beyond me, but it was absorbing and I did find out some amazing facts. For example, that margarine was invented in 1869, when Napoleon III held a competition to find a butter substitute. I also watched smoke being tackled within a transparent catalytic converter and learnt exactly what the carpet on which we all trod was made out of. Meanwhile our 4-year-old amused himself with a hefty slidey contraption demonstrating the slipperiness of surfaces.

"Magical mixtures to shake and colour-changing lights to wonder at"

You'll encounter a great tank full of pink fluid and by pressing buttons you open valves and guide the stuff through pumps and pipes into a reactor vessel. The trick is to operate them in the right order. Next to this is a yellowish solution to try your hand with.

There are lots of screens to watch and computers to give answers to questions that you select. You'll find plenty of these in the new interactive Chemicals for Life gallery – board games, computer quizes and touch screens all combining to trace the evolution of the chemical industry from the 1940's; my son declared it "wicked". Splitting molecules is another experiment to have a go at and our 7-year-old caused a minor explosion as he formed electricity, sending off a spark that ignited the gases he'd separated.

By presenting your hand for analysis you can find out what factor sun screen to buy or if you press your hand against the giant wall thermometer it will reveal your temperature – a stool is provided for children to try this one. Another bit of fun can be had by leaning against black sheets to cause the crystals within to change colour with your body heat. There are Magical Mixtures to shake and colour-changing lights to wonder at. We had a poke around the Living Room, smelling chairs, prodding cushions, fingering the curtains, tapping the bookcases and tables and stroking the wallpaper. This was to guess which things were of man-made materials: a game that keeps getting resurrected now whenever we're out. Going up to the Observatory is a treat in the glass elevator, watching the ground become smaller as the estuary seems wider. At the top you enter a glass-walled room with notices pointing out the industrial sites around.

There's a camera you can spy through, moving it over the viaduct or bridge to relay the scene live on screen. Our pre-schooler loved "filming" a train, but I'll always feel like someone's watching me next time I head for the Wirral! We also had fun in the scented area with its soaps, washing powders and cleaning agents on display, and receptors to stick your nose into to match up smells with pictures. I was fascinated to learn that synthetic coffee scent exists for caterers and that florists can apply the scent of flowers from a spray.

Back downstairs you'll find the Elements Cafe and the souvenir shop full of little scientific bits and pieces. It's easy to get a pushchair round the place and there's a soft play area for toddlers. Excess energy can be run off outside on Spike Island, the site of the old Gossage Works, which you get to by crossing a wooden bridge (watch out for the gaps) over the loch and following a sandy path. There's a Heritage Trail to take you round the park and the St Helens Canal with good views of Fiddler's Ferry. Meanwhile the viaduct and great arc of Runcorn Bridge loom near beckoning you homewards.

Fact File

- ADDRESS: Catalyst, Mersey Road, Widnes, Cheshire
- TELEPHONE: 0151 420 1121
- DIRECTIONS: M62, exit 7, signposted Widnes, or M56, exit 12 to Runcorn Bridge. Follow brown signs
- PUBLIC TRANSPORT: Train to Runcorn Station, walk across the bridge or hop on a bus from station
- DISTANCE: 25 miles
- TRAVEL TIME: 35 minutes
- OPENING: 10.00am-5.00pm daily except Mondays, unless Bank Holiday. Open at 11.00 at weekends
- PRICES: Adults £4.65, children £3.40, under-5's free. Family ticket £13.95
- RESTAURANT FACILITIES: Yes   conc £3.95
- NAPPY CHANGING FACILITIES: Yes
- HIGH CHAIRS: Yes
- DOGS: No
- PUSHCHAIR-FRIENDLY: Yes
- NEARBY: Norton Priory (01928 569895) for woodland gardens, sculptures and bee-keeping demonstrations

Eureka!

WINNER OF NUMEROUS AWARDS, INCLUDING THE MOST PARENT-friendly venue in 1995, Eureka! is a hands-on museum with a science theme designed especially for children. It's a registered charity and very accessible, so come on, hop on a train (it's right next to the station), fill up the car or climb on the bus. You've no excuses to miss this one and you don't need to pack much as it's a child-oriented haven.

Follow the yellow brick road (yes, really) past the Health Trail to the entrance. Once inside a kaleidoscope of colours opens up. The whole museum is jam-packed with specially-designed exhibits : all of them to be touched and, in many cases, actually put to use by the children. It is divided into different areas, each designed to allow exploring and learning: such as "touch", "technology" or "geography", but the noise level demonstrates that the kids are finding their lessons far from boring.

Our favourite was the Town Square, where the kids withdrew 'money' from the bank, selected groceries in M&S (having learned about the production and nutritional information of their purchases) and paid for them at the electronic till. Alternatively, they could have chosen to be a 'bank clerk' with access to the safe, or perhaps the 'check-out assistant', scanning the wares and taking the money.

"Jam-packed with specially-designed exhibits to be touched and put to use"

Outside there are jobs for workmen and women, or there's the Post Office where uniforms, parcels and letters await willing couriers. Our Postman Pat-mad 2-year-old duly donned a peak cap, long tunic and enormous sack and delivered mail to the various parts of Eureka! to his little heart's content. Children love joining in the role play, and there are plenty of staff to help things along. It's a great place to get lost in imagination.

In the Garage aspiring mechanics can have a go and

there's a house complete with transparent toilet and exhibits to show how gas, electricity and water enter. You know all those questions kids ask that you just can't answer? Well, they can find out for themselves in the new Things Gallery!

Upstairs meet Scoot, the robot. He'll introduce you to his Me and My Body trail and you can note your own details as you work round the interactive exhibits. Once you've climbed behind the giant skull, sat within an enormous mouth and watched machines demonstrating how your insides work, you can enter your vital statistics into Scoot's computer to see how many previous visitors share your characteristics, but don't worry – the emphasis is on how unique we all are!

So do you want to read the news or would you rather be behind the camera? This choice is offered in the media communications section. Faxes, telephones and videophones are all here to be tampered with in the name of discovery. There's a yacht to steer (life jackets on for authenticity) and a book tree to climb too.

Outside in the Park you can see (and hear!) a rap 3D audio-visual presentation inside the Hazard Dome, a yellow futuristic dome which gives an unmissable ten minutes on accident prevention.

The Jungle for under-5's has ball pool, slide, giant jigsaws, soft building shapes, and lots of animals and plants to find. Although some areas, such as the Factory (where you can work a production line), are restricted to older children, younger ones won't run out of things to see and do, as special activities and seasonal themes ensure that no one sits still. The craft area was particularly welcome: its supervised sticky moments with glue or paint giving us grown ups time for a breather, whilst watching someone else scrunch the tissue paper and mop up the spillage.

There's a cafe for hot and cold food, or you can picnic outside. Scientific bits and bobs are to be found in the gift shop. The cloak room is unsupervised so leave cumbersome items at home.

With pre-schoolers it's best to visit during term time as it gets pretty crowded when school's out, although some mid-week afternoons are half price which is handy if you live within a short distance. Give yourselves plenty of time if you can, as there's absolutely loads to do here!

Fact File

- ADDRESS: Eureka! The Museum For Children, Discovery Road, Halifax, Yorkshire
- TELEPHONE: 01422 330012
- DIRECTIONS: M62 to junction 24, follow Halifax signs, brown signs will then lead you to Eureka!
- PUBLIC TRANSPORT: Next to railway station with direct trains from Manchester and Blackpool. Regular buses available too
- DISTANCE: 30 miles
- TRAVEL TIME: 45 minutes
- OPENING: Daily 10.00am-5.00pm
- PRICES: Adults (and over-12's) £5.25, children £4.25, under-3's free. Family ticket £16.95
- RESTAURANT FACILITIES: Yes
- NAPPY CHANGING FACILITIES: Yes
- HIGH CHAIRS: Yes
- DOGS: No
- PUSHCHAIR-FRIENDLY: Yes
- NEARBY: Shibden Hall & Park (01422 352246), a 15th century house, horse-drawn carriage museum and extensive grounds

Leighton Hall

Upstairs, downstairs and in my Lady's chamber!

IF YOU LIKE A GOOD GOSSIP THEN PAY A VISIT TO LEIGHTON HALL to hear of all the calamities its walls have witnessed and take in the curiosities left behind. Just a pebble's throw from Morecambe Bay, this enormous castellated stately home gives you the opportunity to come and look round someone else's house. You're treated to a friendly guided tour, including the history of the Hall and who has lived here and told all about the furniture, as well as what goes on within its walls today. The emphasis is on the fact that you're in someone's actual home, rather than a museum, and you might notice the correspondence left behind the clock on the mantelpiece or other tell-tale "lived in" signs.

The tour lasts about 45 minutes, starting in the entrance hall. You can leave buggies here, if you wish, although you may be able to take them round if you don't mind a few stairs. You'll get a lively, informal talk all about the personalities that once dwelled here and their interesting lives. Through the centuries this included an unfortunate imprisonment; an eccentric man who allowed the Hall to go to rack and ruin; bankruptcy; a dog named Badger who chewed off the leg from the Gillow Daisy Table and the 14-year-old servant girl who was summoned each night to the Master's bedroom in order to snuff out his candle.

These accounts were delivered with humour and affection and, whenever purchases of the estate were mentioned, a small voice from the front (where the children had been invited to cluster) informed all and sundry that his Mum and Dad were trying to sell their house, too. As the tour went on, details of our personal lives were further loudly imparted and our 4-year-old even demanded the guide to explain what she was doing in the house if she didn't live there! All this was taken in good spirit and the children were allowed to sit on the grand antique furniture. The Carving chairs they duly graced had been used by a visiting Beatrix Potter to illustrate The Tale Of Squirrel Nutkin. The table dated from 1671, had telescopic properties and was adorned in sparkling silver which had our baby transfixed.

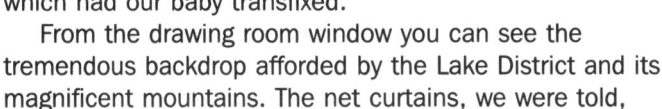

From the drawing room window you can see the tremendous backdrop afforded by the Lake District and its magnificent mountains. The net curtains, we were told, had been left by Granada TV after the filming of a Sherlock Holmes episode. Other house-keeping secrets were revealed as we trailed through the Hall, the origins of fire screens, for example, being to prevent melting of the wax make-up once worn by the gentry. Life for the servants was conjured up as we took in the 23 bells and heard how each one had a different tone which the unfortunate maid would have to decipher.

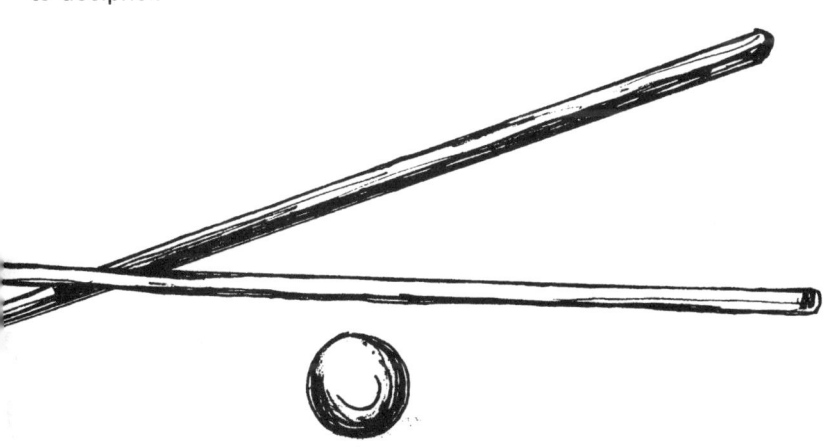

"The table had telescopic properties and was adorned in sparkling silver"

☞ It is in the servants' quarters that the cafe can be found today, selling scrumptious lunches and teas, and allowing you to genuinely experience life below stairs.

The woodlands provide much fun and you can follow the pathways or immerse yourselves in the trees. There's the maze to have a go at, quite a puzzle, although it's not a high-bordered one so the kids can scamper along without the worry of getting lost. There is also a play area in the form of a dragon!

The gardens are near the Hall, very pretty and fragrant. Further afield is an expanse of grass and tree-dotted area, where you can see birds of prey who fly each fine afternoon at 3.30pm for visitors.

Fact File

- ADDRESS: Leighton Hall, Carnforth, Lancashire
- TELEPHONE: 01524 734474
- DIRECTIONS: M6 to junction 35, and the A6. Signposted
- PUBLIC TRANSPORT: None
- DISTANCE: 60 miles
- TRAVEL TIME: One hour 30 minutes
- OPENING: May to end September, daily except Mondays and Saturdays, 2.00pm-5.00pm. 11.30am-5.00pm during August
- PRICES: Adults £3.60, children £2.40, under-5's free. Family ticket £11.00
- RESTAURANT FACILITIES: Yes
- NAPPY CHANGING FACILITIES: No
- HIGH CHAIRS: No
- DOGS: Outside only
- PUSHCHAIR-FRIENDLY: Outside only
- NEARBY: Levens Hall (01539 560321) near Lancaster has an historic house, topiary gardens and steam collection

Martin Mere Wildfowl & Wetland Centre

So he went with a quack, and a waddle and a quack

IF YOUR LEGS AND PRAM WHEELS NEED A STRETCH THIS IS A GREAT place to land. Martin Mere is a spacious area attracting many species of wild bird who settle for a season or two and do their thing for an admiring public. There's lots of information, activities laid on for the kids, and you can eat in the restaurant or share a picnic with some of the curious feathered visitors outside.

See Australian black swans gliding by eucalyptus trees and Chilean flamingos strutting their stuff along the pampas grass. There's an Oriental theme where koi carp, rhododendrons and bamboo set the scene, and a breath of fresh air among the North American pines.

"In Spring the air is filled with bird song and you will see flurries of activity as nesting becomes centre-stage"

We started off with food in 'The Pink Foot Pantry', where the menu has ornithological titles and the lake is easily viewed through wide windows. Good healthy stuff is offered with plenty for shivering bird-spotters in need of something warm.

A veranda runs alongside the restaurant to a small educational area where jigsaws big and small, books, and craft activities can be enjoyed by the youngsters (some for a small charge). On summer weekends stories are read outside and food is given for little ones to feed whichever beaked character waddles by. The staff are helpful and friendly and readily answer questions.

If you want to sit indoors and watch the goings-on there is a viewing gallery and further afield are a number of hides from where you can gaze around the expanse of countryside unspotted by shy birds. You may find a quiz trail has been laid on or a special theme for the children to involve themselves in – things vary with the seasons as the birds dictate what there is to see and do.

This is a good place whatever the time of year. A languid air hung over when we went during a long dry spell and many birds were in the undergrowth to keep cool. Although an uneventful time on the ornithological calendar there were plenty of activities for children in the Visitors Centre and they had fun making badges.

If we'd dropped by later in the year we would have encountered a very different place: in mid September the first of the geese arrive to stir up the slumber, followed by a steady stream of ducks and Bewick swans to add further chaos, whilst the trees turn to gold and orange before shedding masses of leaves for anoraked children to kick about. During winter kids can don gloves and wellies to run along bare pathways, delight in the swans gliding on a floodlit lake, or lurk in the heated hides. The Hawaiian Nene hatches its young early in the year which, as this is an endangered species of goose, is a celebrated event. If you're in need of a refreshing day out to break up the claustrophobia of the Christmas hols this is one to consider.

As spring advances the colour comes back into the Wetlands and the migrating birds set off whilst the resident female birds (and human visitors) are treated to the sight of richly-plumed suitors. The air is filled with the sound of bird song and you will see flurries of activity as nesting becomes centre-stage. The black swans are amongst the first to hatch their chicks and flamingos can be observed upon clay piles. Children will love to explore the many nesting sites. Binoculars will be handy for this and can be hired for £1.00 with a £20.00 deposit.

From about June the glory of family life can be readily seen as all the chicks are coached in their bird life skills. Our son still talks about the fluffy balls scampering about on "inside out legs" a couple of years ago and watching the flamingos this year we wondered which ones had been those chicks.

When you tire of following the trails around there is a a playground, or you could watch your own chicks get to grips with dipping for bugs in the Pondzone and examining their catch under microscopes alongside.

Fact File

- ADDRESS: Martin Mere Wildfowl & Wetland Centre, Fish Lane, Burscough, Lancashire
- TELEPHONE: 01704 895181
- DIRECTIONS: Junction 27 off M6, signposted also from M61 and M58. Situated off A59 with brown signs to guide you
- PUBLIC TRANSPORT: New Lane station is a 15-minute walk (trains from Wigan)
- DISTANCE: 30 miles
- TRAVEL TIME: 45 minutes
- OPENING: Daily 9.30am-5.30pm (4.30pm in winter)
- PRICES: Adults £4.50, children £2.60, under-4's free. Family ticket £11.75
- RESTAURANT FACILITIES: Yes
- NAPPY CHANGING FACILITIES: Yes
- HIGH CHAIRS: Yes
- DOGS: No
- PUSHCHAIR-FRIENDLY: Yes
- NEARBY: Rufford Old Hall (01704 821254) a National Trust house & garden

National Railway Museum

YES – IT'S A LONG WAY TO TRAVEL FOR A DAY OUT, BUT THIS IS A marvellous place, worth a full day's visit and you can make a treat of it by going there and back on the train, which is quicker than driving. Pace yourselves by interspersing the big trains with spells in the indoor or outdoor playgrounds, and save your visit to the superb interactive Magician's Road until spirits are in need of a revival.

The museum consists of two enormous halls, the South Hall and the Great Hall, with a subway between where you can leave coats in lockers. There is also an outdoor area, South Yard, with miniature railway rides, a play area and Magician's Road. As you go in ask about special events: on our visit we watched a turntable demonstration and an excellent 20-minute play about railway navvies.

In the Great Hall begin at the huge central turntable. This is operated twice a day and can turn the biggest of engines, manoeuvring the locomotives on and off for work or storage.

> **"Twenty four gleaming engines stand around the central turntable like the rays of the sun"**

Twenty four gleaming engines stand around it like the rays of the sun, a spectacular sight. Look for the engine which you can walk right underneath, peering up at its great chains and mechanisms, and the engine which has been sliced in half. There are steps alongside many of the carriages on display, allowing you to have a good peer inside. We particularly enjoyed the Royal Mail display, where the children tried a pneumatic pump, felt the weight of mail bags, sorted letters and did a computer quiz.

On the opposite side of the hall you'll find a model

railway with engines tootling round a large track layout. There are steps up so that even toddlers get a good view. Our two-year-old loved it and would have stayed all day watching the trains going in and out of tunnels. Nearby is an interactive area of railway toys and games, and don't forget to have a look at Mallard alongside, the gleaming holder of the world speed record for a steam loco (126 mph).

Over in the South Hall there are more trains to admire, some of which you can climb on. There is a large exhibition of Royal carriages, including one used by Queen Victoria. The interiors are suitably plush, and waxwork figures inside help children imagine what it was like for such wealthy passengers.

Outside in South Yard there are steam and diesel locos and working replicas of Stephenson's Rocket and Iron Duke. These are operated at weekends and holidays when you can have a free ride. If none of the big engines is going there is often a miniature one to sit astride and chuff up and down a short track. You may need to queue as it only carries a few passengers at a time, but alongside is a children's playground and plenty of benches.

Then there is the excellent Magician's Road to visit, an active learning gallery explaining some of the principles behind railway operations. Undoubtedly the biggest hit with our party, do leave yourself enough time for this. There are many practical and ingenious things to try, from building a bridge, working a signal box and wheeltapping, to 'driving' an Intercity train, pushing tubs of coal and laying a miniature track in a battle against the clock.

The restaurant in the middle of South Hall has meals and snacks, or you can picnic in the area next to the indoor playground. The museum shop sells all kinds of souvenirs, some at pocket money prices. Take note of the toilet locations: in the Great Hall and next to the shop, but none in the South Hall or South Yard, and it is quite a long walk back from Magician's Road to the central toilets.

Fact File

- ADDRESS: National Railway Museum, Leeman Road, York, N. Yorkshire
- TELEPHONE: 01904 621261
- DIRECTIONS: M62 and A1 north, then A64 into York. In the city centre follow signs to station and then museum. Car park at north entrance
- PUBLIC TRANSPORT: Trains from Piccadilly station to York about every 30 minutes. 10-minute walk from station
- DISTANCE: 65 miles
- TRAVEL TIME: 1 hour 30 minutes
- OPENING: Daily 10.00am-6.00pm. Last admission one hour earlier
- PRICES: Adults £4.95, children £3.50, under-4's free, family £14.50
- RESTAURANT FACILITIES: Yes
- NAPPY CHANGING FACILITIES: Yes
- HIGH CHAIRS: Yes
- DOGS: No
- PUSHCHAIR-FRIENDLY: Yes
- NEARBY: York has other museums and attractions. Try walking on the city walls for a change

Port Sunlight Village

Take a wander back in time and around the village of Port Sunlight, over its pretty hump-backed bridge and along the stone monuments to the Lady Lever Art Gallery. Pop into Christ's Church where the founder of the village and his wife now lie for eternity and see the dazzling stained glass. Assemble on a bench or spread a blanket over the grass for a picnic in a perfect setting. It's a good place to visit in all weathers as there are plenty of places to shelter in if the weather turns bad.

It was near the end of the last century when William Hesketh Lever expanded his soap manufacturing to the Wirral. He turned the surrounding, marshy land into a village for his workforce, employing almost thirty architects for the task. You will marvel at the end result; row upon row of pretty cottages, some mock-Tudor, others with colonnades and more with decorative outcrops. Their leaded windows glint in the sun as a multitude of birdlife completes the scene with regular choruses.

> "Neat pathways edge the intricate houses and run along the dell beneath the bridge"

To cap it all the fragrance of soap wafts around from the factory – pack strong flavoured food into your picnic to counteract this, although it does add a touch of aromatherapy to the unwinding process!

Visit the Heritage Centre to learn all about this curious little haven. It has a scaled-down model of the village and my eldest pointed out a tiny red car, just where we'd parked ours (the foresight of which amazed his little brother!). We played spot what's in mum's cupboard with the display of products currently manufactured by Lever and I pointed out the dated packages that my grandmother favoured. There are photographs depicting the early years, as well as a royal visit, and some of the old architects' plans are on the wall. You can see a dolls-house-sized model of an 1930's cottage or peer into the alcove where a living-room has been reconstructed. We bought postcards and the kids had fun emblazoning them with the custom-made ink stamps. There's a gift selection and tourist information point, too.

Just next door, within the mock-Tudor cottagey walls, is a Nat West bank, complete with outside automatic cash point! Adjacent there's a post office and opposite is Port Sunlight Station, with its gracefully-aged facade blending perfectly with the surroundings.

There are grassy spaces everywhere as the buildings are constructed in short terraces around a green and neat pathways edge the intricate houses and run along the dell beneath the bridge. The trees shed enormous golden leaves during the autumn which carpet the greens and pathways to the delight of small wellington-clad feet.

Get a leaflet from the Heritage Centre which, for 50p, will guide you round, past Lever House, Hesketh and Hulme Halls and the other scenic buildings. There are some decorative paved steps by the bridge but the main areas are pushchair friendly. You will marvel at the sight from The Causeway, as monuments and rows of flowers lead the way to the domed Art Gallery. There are free fact sheets available from the centre and quiz sheets, including one for younger visitors. Try the Art Gallery, if only briefly, as children enjoy spotting detail in pictures. We found the restaurant there too sophisticated for our brood, so it's best to picnic or try the pub food on offer at the Bridge Inn.

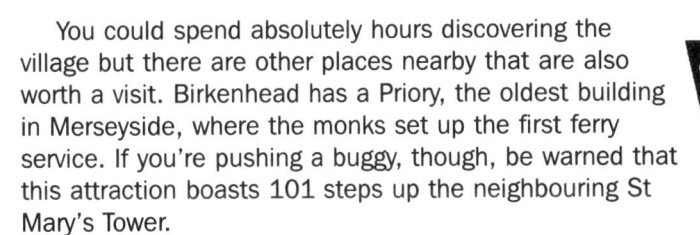

You could spend absolutely hours discovering the village but there are other places nearby that are also worth a visit. Birkenhead has a Priory, the oldest building in Merseyside, where the monks set up the first ferry service. If you're pushing a buggy, though, be warned that this attraction boasts 101 steps up the neighbouring St Mary's Tower.

Another worthwhile visit is Warships, along the Dock Road at Wallasey. Unfortunately it's impossible to get a pushchair round the Falklands veteran, HMS Plymouth, never mind down the hatches of the Onyx Submarine, but if baby can be entertained elsewhere, it's an interesting port to call at. (I toured these vessels with bated breath as I watched my 4-year-old negotiate the many steps, so be careful on board with a toddler). England's first park, Birkenhead Park, which was used as a model for New York's Central, would suit younger families and this is signposted, as all the attractions are. If you're coming to the Wirral via the City of Liverpool then a drive through one of the tunnels will be an extra treat for your passengers and even the return journey can be looked forward to!

Fact File

- ADDRESS: Port Sunlight Village Heritage Centre, 95 Greendale Road, Port Sunlight, Wirral, Merseyside
- TELEPHONE: 0151 644 6466
- DIRECTIONS: M53 off M56 and follow signs, or through Queensway tunnel from Liverpool
- PUBLIC TRANSPORT: Trains from Liverpool or Chester and regular buses
- DISTANCE: 45 miles
- TRAVEL TIME: 1 hour 15 minutes
- OPENING: 10.00am-4.00pm daily from April to October, weekdays only the rest of the year
- PRICES: Adults 40p, children 20p, under-5's free
- RESTAURANT FACILITIES: Yes (Art Gallery)
- NAPPY CHANGING FACILITIES: Yes (Art Gallery)
- HIGH CHAIRS: No
- DOGS: Outside only
- PUSHCHAIR-FRIENDLY: Yes
- NEARBY: Boat Museum (0151 355 5017) at Ellesmere Port

The Great Outdoors

Beeston Castle

She marched them up to the top of the hill . . .

PEPPERING THE COUNTRYSIDE OF CHESHIRE ARE A NUMBER OF castles left behind by the Normans, used for defence in further skirmishes, battered by the British climate and plundered and vandalised through the centuries. Like Beeston, now owned by English Heritage, many are at last being lovingly tended by their keepers. The armies that turn out today carry cameras, binoculars, butty boxes and disposable nappies. Our's did, anyway.

> "The armies that turn out today carry cameras, binoculars, butty boxes and disposable nappies"

And it was something of a battle to reach the summit of Beeston's well chosen hill. I felt as though I was wearing chain-mail body stocking as we forged onwards and upwards to reach our conquest. But it was worth it. So pack up the picnic, get out your stout walking shoes, root out the kids' kite and take a deep breath.

At the entrance at the bottom of the hill is a souvenir shop and museum with archaeological finds and information about Beeston and its role in the Civil War. You can get hot drinks and snacks from the vending machine here. It's a good idea to use the toilets here too before the climb as there are none in the castle itself. There are, however, lots of bushes! No baby changing room or cafe, though so you really are getting away from day to day life. At peak visiting times there's a hot dog van in the car park but come prepared in case of disappointment.

We took the middle path up the hill and stopped for a breather on a thoughtfully-provided bench, after about 15 minutes. Here you will see that a path has been trodden either side and these both lead to the remains at the top. If you take the left you'll find the going a bit easier. In our ignorance of this we didn't and it was a good half hour before we arrived panting at the drawbridge.

Looking down you can see the old stone ramp which used to meet a small wooden bridge. Now there is a newer bridge, leading onto the plateau where the rocky ground is bordered by what's left of the castle walls. Don't try to get the buggy round *this* crazy paving, and hold onto those toddlers! It was a blustery day when we braved this trip and up on top the wind gusted round. No wonder there's not much left to see! There are rooms to walk into, from whose slitted arrow holes you can survey the green and brown land that men through history have scrutinised for signs of danger. Look out for rare Peregrine falcons helping to guard the craggy tops, or nesting ravens, unusual in this part of the country. The scenery from the Castle is glorious and if you look over the bridge a neighbouring fort can be seen. Imagine what must have gone on in the valley between!

We made our way back down the outer pathway, passing look out points, pieces of wall and steps. We even came across a very old well which has a tree growing from one of its sides. The raw, unfussed nature of Beeston is invigorating and you can see the original craftsmanship in the remains, filling in the gaps of time with your imagination. There's no one to frown at little tourists as they trespass on lawns and touch exhibits. You can shout, scamper about, run and jump, throw tantrums and whine for more chocolate as much as you like. We did!

At the bottom we congratulated ourselves, checked the suspension on the push-chair and purchased supplies from the shop. There is a flatter grassy area here with benches, ideal for picnics. Nearby are some caves, which you can reach by sliding down a wilderness (as our 7-year-old did) or by walking down some steps. Their entrances are railed off but it's quite something to press your forehead against the bars and stare into the darkness. The children were wary about bears so we continued our walk, searching for dinosaur fossils and mammoth tusks, arrow heads and wild boar.

Fact File

- ADDRESS: Beeston Castle, Beeston, Cheshire
- TELEPHONE: 01829 260464
- DIRECTIONS: Junction 17 off M6, follow A534 to Nantwich, and on west to the A49 Chester to Whitchurch road. Just off the A49 in the Chester direction
- PUBLIC TRANSPORT: None
- DISTANCE: 50 miles
- TRAVEL TIME: 1 hour
- OPENING: Daily 10.00am-6.00pm (summer), 10.00am-4.00pm (winter)
- PRICES: Adults £2.70, children £1.40, under-5's free. English Heritage members free
- RESTAURANT FACILITIES: No
- NAPPY CHANGING FACILITIES: Yes
- HIGH CHAIRS: No
- DOGS: Yes
- PUSHCHAIR-FRIENDLY: Just about
- NEARBY: Stapeley Water Gardens (01270 628628) Nantwich for The Palms tropical oasis gardens

Capesthorne Hall

*Curiouser and curiouser!
cried Alice*

A PAIR OF FLAT SHOES IS A MUST FOR CAPESTHORNE, NOT JUST because stilettos are banned inside the Hall but also as there is so much walking to be done around the grounds and in the woods. The Hall has a collection of paintings and sculptures as well as exquisite furniture but the wide open spaces outside are the main attraction for people with children.

We started by circling the Hall, wheeling the buggy along paths and peering into the Chapel. This is most attractive and still in use. There is a beautiful mosaic and intricately carved wood and stone. You can't go right inside but all can be seen from the door. Not far away the children discovered small tombstones where the family pets have been laid to rest beneath the trees. Poor Fergus has been in this spot since 1882! There is also a pretty little

> **"We came to a lake with clumps of four-foot-high rhubarb and dragonflies hovering about"**

remembrance garden for the ancestors of the current owners, with the history of the family illustrated by monuments placed throughout the centuries, right up until the late 1980s.

There are three lakes within the park, one of which is spanned by a spectacular bridge and on a sunny day the reflection of its many arches is breathtaking.

Deciding to explore the woods we left the well-kept lawns and neat pathways in favour of shady trees and bumpy hillocks. Our elder two forged ahead whilst we dawdled with the buggy and they soon reported back that they'd found a bridge. This is tiny and near the ice house, leading you over a brook and deeper into the trees. There

☞ were lots of rustling sounds, produced by birds, perhaps, or even small mammals.

Eventually we came to a lake with clumps of four-foot-high rhubarb on its banks and dragonflies hovering about. Twigs snapped underfoot and birds sang all around as we went in single file through the jungle. We arrived at a long wall in which is a row of doors. Curiously, there was nothing on the other side of the wall and we half expected a white rabbit with a pocket watch to appear! Presently we reached a padlocked gate and retraced our steps.

Back near the Hall is the Garden Tea Room where afternoon tea can be taken in a conservatory or on the terrace. There is a broad ledge in the Ladies loo which is wide enough for nappy manoeuvres. Just outside here is Lewis Carroll wallpaper which we thought was nicely in keeping with the pointless doors and enormous rhubarb!

If you go inside the Hall you'll find the Servants'

Quarters chock-full with photographs, news cuttings, letters, ledgers and personal family memorabilia. With lots of bits and pieces belonging to the current owners, too, it is satisfyingly voyeuristic to look round! Upstairs are large rooms with many works of art on the walls; these are roped off but the barriers weren't enough to contain our over-enthusiastic children.

Capesthorne Hall holds special events periodically throughout the year and, if you enjoy camping, fees for caravans and tents include admission into the garden. You'd certainly wake up to a lovely view.

Fact File

- ADDRESS: Capesthorne Hall, Siddington, near Macclesfield, Cheshire
- TELEPHONE: 01625 861221
- DIRECTIONS: Off the A34, just south of Alderley Edge
- PUBLIC TRANSPORT: None
- DISTANCE: 20 miles
- TRAVEL TIME: 45 minutes
- OPENING: Wednesdays, Sundays and Bank Holidays, from March to October. 12noon-6.00pm (gardens), 1.30pm-3.30pm (Hall)
- PRICES: Garden only £2.50 adult, £1.00 child. All-inclusive admission £4.50 adults, £2.00 children, under-5's free. Family ticket £9.50
- RESTAURANT FACILITIES: Yes
- NAPPY CHANGING FACILITIES: Yes
- HIGH CHAIRS: Yes
- DOGS: Outside only
- PUSHCHAIR-FRIENDLY: Yes
- NEARBY: Jodrell Bank (01477 571339) to see how the space telescope works. Over-5's may enjoy the Planetarium

Chatsworth House

Meandering along the twisty driveway to Chatsworth House, we were following in the footsteps of Daniel Defoe, although I doubt that he had his two point five kids in tow. This splendid building has been open to the public ever since its erection in the mid 16th century, although probably never before in such a well-organised way. It now offers splendid gardens with sculptures and fountains, an opulent and artistically-bestowed house full of history, a farm, adventure playground, gift shops and an exquisite restaurant set in the old Carriage House.

There are over 100 acres and five miles of footpath to follow in the garden, so bring the buggy! The breathtaking Cascade, a beautiful temple from which water springs elegantly to flow gracefully down a series of wide steps, makes you realise what a magical setting you're in. We romped about the stone figures dotted here and there, admired the historical features, got lost in The Maze and picked up a few gardening tips in the Kitchen, Rose and Cottage gardens. On Summer Sundays a brass band playing makes an amble round the gardens even more enjoyable. Further afield, for those who really like to stretch their legs, blow away the cobwebs and get away from it all, are the 1000 acres of parkland which Capability Brown landscaped, or 5 miles of marked trails through the woods behind the house.

"There is so much to see in the garden that you will have no trouble filling your day"

You can herd the kids over to the working farm too, where a non-sentimental, matter-of-fact approach is taken to teach city-dwellers the realities of country life. It is a compact area where pigs, cattle, hens, ducks, trout, sheep, horses and goats, can be seen going about their business. The ultimate uses of the animals are explained along with their feeding and breeding habits. Children can feed the trout, play on a tractor and absorb the hustle and bustle around them. At 3.30pm each day there's a milking demonstration, given with a microphone so everyone can hear, with plenty of time and encouragement at the end for questions. At the height of the visiting season there's a shop and cafe down there too.

From the farm sneak through the secret tunnel into the adventure playground where scramble nets, rope walks, firemen's poles, commando slides, tree houses, the tunnel maze and lots of other logged structures wait to be conquered. There are wood chips over the hilly ground – which our baby enjoyed chewing – and trees all around. We had a heart-stopping moment when our pre-schooler was spotted high up a scramble net, whilst his more sensible older brother had his own silly moment when he heartily led a posse into the woods, to return a good twenty minutes later.

By the entrance to the House itself is the tuck shop, which made a welcome pit stop after a lengthy drive through Cheshire and into Derbyshire. We thought the House, with the Scots Bedrooms, where Mary Queen of Scots spent part of her captivity, and other royal relics would be best left until the children were older. There is so much to see in the garden that you will have no trouble filling your day. Before leaving for home, however, we enjoyed a scrumptious tea in the Carriage House Restaurant, although we had intended to stop at a roadside cafe en route. All agreed that we'd made the right choice.

Fact File

- ADDRESS: Chatsworth House, Bakewell, Derbyshire
- TELEPHONE: 01246 582204
- DIRECTIONS: A6, or M6 junction 19 and A537, via Buxton and on to Bakewell
- PUBLIC TRANSPORT: 25 minute walk through park from Baslow. Bus available
- DISTANCE: 50 miles
- TRAVEL TIME: 1 hour 30 minutes
- OPENING: 11.00am-4.30pm 18 March to 1 November
- PRICES: Garden £3.60 adults, £1.75 children. Farm and playground £3.00 per person. Under-3's free. Extra for House
- RESTAURANT FACILITIES: Yes
- NAPPY CHANGING FACILITIES: Yes
- HIGH CHAIRS: Yes
- DOGS: Garden only, dog park for farm
- PUSHCHAIR-FRIENDLY: Yes
- NEARBY: Peak District National Park

Cholmondeley Castle Gardens

She knelt by the side of the lily pond, and bent her golden head to kiss the frog

THIS PEACEFUL YET DRAMATIC SETTING WILL GIVE THE KIDS' imaginations a stretch, along with their legs. The castle is just like the ones in children's story books; it is up on a hill and has arched windows and battlements. You can't go in the building but on a fine day there's lots of exploring to be done in its landscaped gardens and to complete the day you'll also find a rare breeds farm.

We started by absorbing the delights of the Temple Garden. Walking along its still lake, taking in the bordering plants and lilies, the bridges, pampas grass and ferns, I almost expected Claude Monet to appear on one of the islands, paint brush in hand. Statues and follies, gateways and stone seating, make this a perfect backdrop for spurned lovers to come and lament, or for those in need of artistic inspiration, or even for harassed parents to escape to! It is a beautiful place and surely the envy of many potential Percy Throwers. For me the silent lady who stood so still as she took a secret dip, summed up this tranquil paradise, and even if she had not been a statue, I am sure her conduct would have seemed perfectly in keeping with the magical and feminine atmosphere here. The bridges can be crossed to reach the islands, koi carp swimming gracefully around, and even the kids, their minds filled with fantasies, didn't manage to break the spell.

> "Statues and follies, gateways and stone seating make this a perfect backdrop"

The Rose Garden is prettily laid-out and its scent is matched only by the nearby lavender that courts gently-humming bees. With the gothic castle in the background, these opulently-landscaped gardens make a fitting place for a princess to walk through, a dragon to galumph by, or a buggy-pushing family to trundle along, chocolate-smeared toddlers bringing up the rear. You can have a game of tag beneath the colossal pine trees, explore the cherry tree walk or simply head for the swing and see-saw to give over-worked imaginations a rest.

In the paddocks, a little walk down the farm road, rare breeds of farm animals can be found. The children enjoyed the curious collection of pigs, cows, sheep, Shetland ponies, goats and llamas. There's a tower with steps round the outside that the pygmy goats gambol up and down and in and out of. As we approached the paddocks, a large building came into view which bounced the boys' voices off its old bricked walls, prompting yet more yells and increasingly strange vocals.

The gift shop nestles in the basement of the castle, surrounded by a pretty terrace with a lily pond – keep those baby reins on! On some summer Sundays brass and steel bands can be heard here. We had freshly made sandwiches and cake for tea, before meandering back along the terrace, around the castle, and into our motorised carriage.

Fact File

- ADDRESS: Cholmondeley Castle, Malpas, Cheshire
- TELEPHONE: 01829 720383
- DIRECTIONS: M56 junction 10, and take the A49 in direction of Tarporley and Whitchurch. Signposted off the A49 just beyond Croxton Green
- PUBLIC TRANSPORT: None
- DISTANCE: 45 miles
- TRAVEL TIME: 1 hour 15 minutes
- OPENING: 1 April to 30 September 11.30am-5.00pm Wednesdays, Thursdays, Sundays & Bank Holidays
- PRICES: Adults £2.50, children 75p, under-5's free
- RESTAURANT FACILITIES: Yes
- NAPPY CHANGING FACILITIES: No
- HIGH CHAIRS: No
- DOGS: Yes
- PUSHCHAIR-FRIENDLY: Yes
- NEARBY: Stapeley Water Gardens (01270 628628) in Nantwich for The Palms tropical oasis garden

Delamere Forest

Five, Six, Pick up Sticks!

FOLLOW IN THE FOOTSTEPS OF ROYAL HUNTING PARTIES OF yesteryear, in this most noble and ancient deciduous forest. You'll find plenty of routes through the trees, picnic sites and lots to learn about the forest ecosystem.

If you park your car at the Linmere Park Picnic Area you'll find information boards and route maps set up by Cheshire County Council. It's a good place to start, although you can park in several areas throughout the forest and disappear into the trees. Make sure you remember where you parked your car, though! Stick to the paths with pushchairs and it is quite accessible, although wellies wouldn't go amiss in several places.

Further into the forest, and down the lane from Delamere station is the Forestry Commission Ranger Centre. We headed here first, through trees and up steps onto a road running between a field of cows and the railway. Families on bicycles free-wheeled down the hill as we plodded upwards. You can drive instead but it isn't far.

> **"We came across plenty of acorns, sycamore wings and prickly conker shells"**

Inside the Ranger station you can sit and watch the birds outside in the ponded gardens. There's a drinks machine and toilets nearby and lots of photographs and information leaflets to grab. We had great fun in the education part where there's a feely box for little hands to grope around to guess whether the rough, knobbly contents are twigs, fir cones, pine needles, bark or whatever. As our kids are forever touching and messing with things this went down well.

For the more sophisticated there's a computer which puts you through your paces as a Forest Ranger. It asks lots of questions on how you would design a forest and really brought home the message of the forest's fragile and well-balanced eco-system. There is a display of stuffed woodland animals to intrigue any Farthingwood fanatic, although our children wondered how they could exist in the same glass case so harmoniously. The weather charts make fascinating reading for aspiring meteorologists too.

Take a look at The Stairs of Survival, a four story house where oak trees grow. They start as seeds in its nursery, graduate to the school room upon becoming saplings, and progress further up the stairs through the house before reaching the top as mature oak trees. Their struggles to get this far are described and setbacks lamented, and we could all relate to their story!

Next door the Groundwork Trust (01625 572681) operates a cycle hire service. You can get mountain bikes on a daily or 3-hourly basis and they have baby carriers too. It is open 10.00am-6.00pm weekends from April to October and every day during July and August. If we're ever free of pushchairs and stabilisers it would be a good way to spend a day. There are plenty of picnic spots to choose from and we found a bench near a bin to have lunch, before setting off again to explore the forest. We really enjoyed the liberating feeling of getting away from the tarmac, traffic and bricks of home, and the children found interesting-shaped twigs and occasionally insisted on lugging branches along. It was a hot day and the forest provided welcome shade. It would be a good ramble even on a damp day, as the ground has so much of interest to aspiring naturalists and the smell of wet woodland is very uplifting. Dog owners will find that this is an excellent place to play fetch although Rover might get confused about which one is his stick! Trees of many varieties stretch for the sun and if you leave a path it's a bit like being in a deciduous jungle: I attempted a short cut, and got stuck in thick bracken whilst Dad sensibly stuck to the path with the pushchair.

We came across plenty of acorns, sycamore wings and prickly conker shells. As the kids were wearily climbing into the bath that night, I didn't have to empty their pockets of the usual collections of debris, though, as they'd already decided that the seeds should stay in their nurseries on the forest floor instead!

Fact File

- ADDRESS: Linmere Visitor Centre, Delamere, Cheshire
- TELEPHONE: 01606 889792
- DIRECTIONS: M56 junction 12, to Frodsham. Pick up the B5152 towards Delamere, and turn right into the Forest at Hatchmere
- PUBLIC TRANSPORT: Trains from Manchester, via Chester, to Delamere Station
- DISTANCE: 35 miles
- TRAVEL TIME: 1 hour
- OPENING: Daily 10.30am-4.30pm (Ranger Centre). Entry to forest all times
- PRICES: Free
- RESTAURANT FACILITIES: No
- NAPPY CHANGING FACILITIES: No
- HIGH CHAIRS: No
- DOGS: Yes
- PUSHCHAIR-FRIENDLY: Yes
- NEARBY: Mouldsworth Motor Museum (01928 731781) for cars and motorbike memorabilia

Haigh Hall Park & Craft Centre

THIS IS A SPOT FOR THOSE WHO LIKE TAKING-IN LUNG-FULLS OF AIR, types who'll revel in stretching their limbs around its 250 acres of woods, trampolines, crazy golf, miniature railway, model village and bouncy castle. It's also the perfect outing for those who want to be indoors, having a go at clay model-making, batik, watercolours, stencilling or embossing. Within the grounds of the stately Haigh Hall, a grand looking building that's opened to the public for special occasions, you can be guaranteed a really interesting and varied day out, whatever the weather, and there really should be something here for everyone.

We rolled in on a fresh, November day, and started with a stroll in the wooded areas and walled Walker Gardens. There are a variety of trails to follow and pathways to trek, ranging from a 30-minute amble to a two-hour ramble. We ended up at a big pond that looks like an enormous stone dish, one of the many features of the original grounds that Victorian ladies and gents enjoyed. Everywhere smelt of pine and the sound of crows and rustling leaves gave our surroundings a crisp, end-of-the-year feel.

> **"A number of artists in residence, ever-ready to demonstrate their craft"**

Through the stone arch into the cobbled courtyard, where picnic benches have replaced the sheaves of hay and grooms, we found the old stables and plenty more to do. The information centre and shop is there, providing coloured trail leaflets (free) as well as gift items and pocket money toys. Beyond this is the Gallery, with a number of artists in residence, ever-ready to demonstrate their craft, with no obligation to buy. We came upon an art class, a group of children beavering away in a

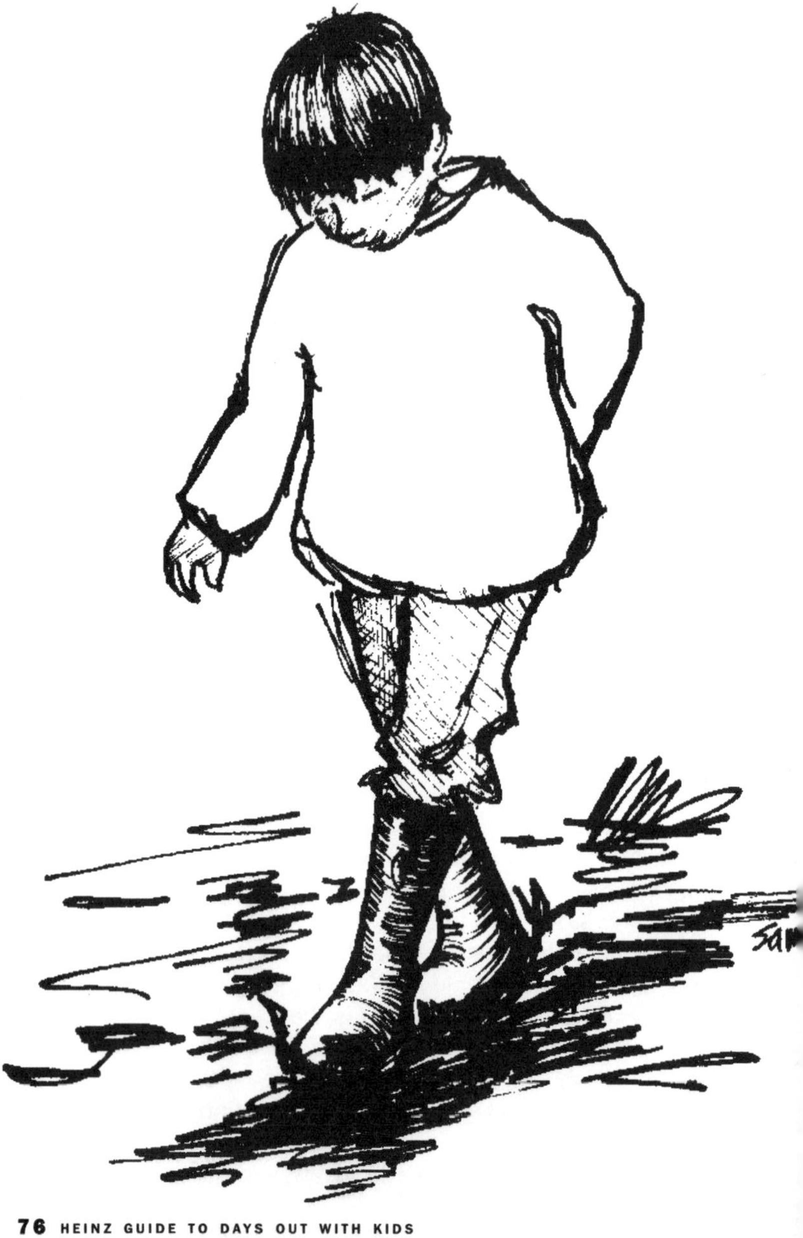

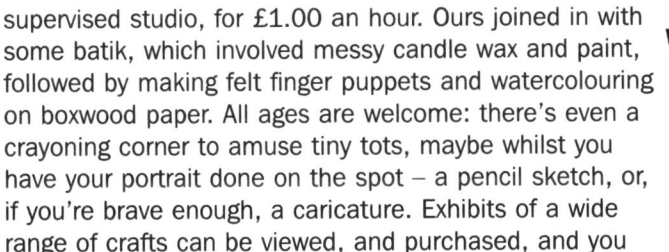

supervised studio, for £1.00 an hour. Ours joined in with some batik, which involved messy candle wax and paint, followed by making felt finger puppets and watercolouring on boxwood paper. All ages are welcome: there's even a crayoning corner to amuse tiny tots, maybe whilst you have your portrait done on the spot – a pencil sketch, or, if you're brave enough, a caricature. Exhibits of a wide range of crafts can be viewed, and purchased, and you can watch many of them being made, so feel free to peer over shoulders.

There's always something different here, as the artists operate on a rota, and the seasons bring their own changes to the woodlands and gardens. From spring onwards there's a bouncy castle, ladybird ride, miniature railway and model village (£2.00 for a Junior Saver ticket giving four rides), and the whole country park is alive with activities. You can join the Ranger Service for a bit of archery, orienteering, rock climbing, cycling, or woodland scrambling, but ring to check and book these in advance.

Fact File

- ADDRESS: Haigh Country Park, Haigh, Wigan, Greater Manchester
- TELEPHONE: 01942 832895
- DIRECTIONS: M61 to junction 6, B5239 to Aspull, then on to Haigh. M6 to junction 27, A49 to Sandish, then B5239 to Haigh
- PUBLIC TRANSPORT: None
- DISTANCE: 25 miles
- TRAVEL TIME: 30 minutes
- OPENING: Daily, dawn until dusk (park). Craft centre 9.30am-4.30pm
- PRICES: Park and craft centre free. Car park 70p
- RESTAURANT FACILITIES: Yes
- NAPPY CHANGING FACILITIES: Yes
- HIGH CHAIRS: Yes
- DOGS: Yes (not craft centre)
- PUSHCHAIR-FRIENDLY: Yes
- NEARBY: Wigan Pier (01942 323666)

Lever Park

THIS WAS MY OLD STOMPING GROUND, BOTH IN NAPPIES AND BIKING leathers, as well as that of the late Lord Leverhulme, who spent much of his leisure time away from Port Sunlight enjoying the design and construction of this most exotic of gardens. After decades of neglect and vandalism, it has been taken over by North West Water Authority and its overgrown secrets of lawns, Japanese garden, pools, waterfalls, terraces, bridges, and pathways rediscovered. It still looks marvellously wild, however, and will inspire anyone with a leaning towards myths and magic, whilst those with an interest in its true history and architectural relics can follow a trail to decipher just what *is* that tiled flooring doing out here in the grass, and exactly *why* the Pigeon Tower is perched innocently atop of all the rugged splendour.

Apart from the sprawling foundations that you can trace through the conquering vegetation, the most impressive buildings to be seen standing today are the 17th century Cruck barns, curiously shaped like Toblerones; one of them is the Great House Barn Information Centre and cafe you see as you drive in. Next you'll see that you have quite a hike in store, up and over to the terraced gardens that await. This is where buggies should be left folded and baby slings and sturdy shoes put on, as there are far too many steps, dips and hollows to negotiate with wheels. Although it is possible to drive up to the top of the gardens, it's still not a place for the faint-legged. Be warned – there are hundreds of steps here – your thigh muscles will be in for a serious workout!

> "There are follies galore for small explorers"

Kids, however, will love running and jumping around the castellated ruins, shooting imaginary arrows at foes, and lurking behind the many corners and bushes that make the ruins and parkland traditional family fun. Something like the opening scene in *Dragonheart*, there are follies galore for small explorers to yell their heads off about, without curators or keepers yelling back.

Pick up a trail leaflet from the Great House Barn. They cost 25p, and there are a number of different routes to follow. Our favourites are the Terraced and Japanese

Gardens, where you'll find turrets and battlements and oodles of curiosities. The ballroom, around which William Lever presumably whirled, is still in evidence – a circular arrangement of stones marking its foundations – as are other parts of his long-gone residence. There are the cherries, currants and blackberries originally planted in the kitchen garden, while more surprising vegetation can be seen near the Japanese garden. All in all there is plenty to discover, and you should all enjoy piecing together the history of the gardens like time detectives (that's if you're not too busy picnicing or hiding and seeking).

It's a good place to visit at any time of the year, gloves and wellies permitting. In winter the ruins may be transformed by the white coating of frost or snow (concealing The Snow Queen within perhaps?), although the wind can be bracing, and slopes and steps may become slippery. In milder weather, it's just the ticket for a free family outing, with fresh air, exercise and brilliantly tatty surroundings to wander in.

You can picnic anywhere in the Park, but you'll find benches down by the Great House Barn, as well as a craft shop and other facilities.

Fact File

- ADDRESS: Lever Park, Rivington Lane, Horwich, Bolton, Lancashire
- TELEPHONE: 01204 691549
- DIRECTIONS: M61 to junction 6, go on to Horwich and follow signs
- PUBLIC TRANSPORT: About 2 miles from Adlington Station (taxis available). Hourly bus from Leigh or from Bolton to Park
- DISTANCE: 20 miles
- TRAVEL TIME: 30 minutes
- OPENING: Anytime. Information centre closed Monday and Tuesday
- PRICES: Free
- RESTAURANT FACILITIES: Yes
- NAPPY CHANGING FACILITIES: Yes
- HIGH CHAIRS: Yes
- DOGS: Yes
- PUSHCHAIR-FRIENDLY: No
- NEARBY: Smithills Hall, Bolton (01204 841265)

Tatton Park

TATTON PARK IS SOME PLACE. TO TAKE IN THE GARDENS, TROT round the Farm, visit the Medieval Hall, tour the Mansion and still have time for lunch in the restaurant or an adventure in the playground it's worth planning a two-day visit (for which Explorer tickets are available). You can pay for each attraction individually too. There is certainly plenty outside in the gardens and woods to occupy a whole day.

The grazing deer that flank the long driveway had the children enchanted before we reached the parking area and, as they spotted the huge play area near the car park, we had to start there. It has wobbly planks, swinging tyres, tight ropes and all the adventurous equipment imaginable. Bribe them away if you can: there's loads more to explore.

The splendid gardens extend round behind the Mansion and are full of fascinating features: bridges, two lakes, opulent flower beds, shrubs, trees with wooden and stone benches all blending in nicely. It's easy to negotiate a buggy round. There are elegantly-arched wrought iron gates, an Orangery and tropical house and a sweeping Italian terrace. We frolicked around the Giant

"Giant American Redwoods, a Japanese garden and a Victorian Maze"

American Redwoods, peeked at the Japanese garden and had a brief game of tag round the fort, before arriving at the Victorian Maze. Our eldest is still crowing that he was the only one to find his way to the middle – my energy was channelled into rescuing our lost four-year-old and I was glad just to find him!

The Stableyard has a garden shop, gift shop, loos, tuck shop and glass-fronted carriage house. You'll find a tractor waiting here for passengers to hop on board for a 50p hour-long ride through the woods, or short horse-and-carriage rides are available too.

Inside the Mansion are all sorts of artistic and historic delights, which we gave a miss in favour of a quick look round The Medieval Old Hall, which is a large, smoky, unlit hall with central hearth and high table. There's an enthralling story of its history during the one-hour tour, which includes an audio-visual show. It is particularly good for older children.

Home Farm is delightfully informal and you're able to potter about in your own time between the cow shed and piggery. We came across a piglet with the same age and name as our daughter! There's plenty of vintage machinery about and as we rumbled our buggy over the cobbles we kept encountering narrow tram lines which we realised later came from the Mill.

More history is revealed when you step in to the 1930's cottage. You can walk around the cosy but poky living room and, if you see a cat on the arm chair let me warn you that it isn't stuffed – it gave us quite a surprise! Upstairs are children's toys and other bits and pieces, whereas next door the farm offices are recaptured with antique typewriters and a turn of the century WC. Trophies and rosettes remind visitors that Tatton Dale's agricultural excellence was renowned, whilst a current gas bill reminded me that the place is still classed as 'working'.

Next to this building enormous horses nod their heads out of stable doors. More horses can be found at the main stables where you can see a demonstration of equine management at 2.00pm daily. They also offer rides around the paddock for 50p.

Fact File

- ADDRESS: Tatton Park, Knutsford, Cheshire
- TELEPHONE: 01565 750250
- DIRECTIONS: M6 junction 19 or M56 junction 8 - follow the brown signs
- PUBLIC TRANSPORT: 10-minute walk from Knutsford Station to Knutsford Gate, bringing you into the Park. A further two mile walk to the main attractions
- DISTANCE: 15 miles
- TRAVEL TIME: 30 minutes
- OPENING: 1 April to end September; park open daily 10.00am-7.00pm, gardens, mansion, Old Hall and farm Tuesday-Sunday 12noon-4.00pm. In winter park and gardens open Tuesday-Sunday 11.00am-5.00pm, and farm open Sundays 11.30am-4.00pm
- PRICES: Entry to Park £3.00 per car. Each attraction individually charged (from £2.50 adults and £1.50 children). All-inclusive Explorer tickets available
- RESTAURANT FACILITIES: Yes
- NAPPY CHANGING FACILITIES: Yes
- HIGH CHAIRS: Yes
- DOGS: Yes
- PUSHCHAIR-FRIENDLY: Yes
- NEARBY: Hillside Ornamental Fowl (01565 873282)

Somewhat Historical

Crewe Railway Age

Man and boy, my father too, and his father before him . . .

SITUATED IN THE CENTRE OF CREWE, A TOWN THAT GREW UP OUT OF the railways in the last century, The Railway Age is easy to find and doesn't need the sun to shine for an enjoyable day out as many interesting things are indoors. The history of Crewe and all things rail are displayed. This is one for real train buffs as you can have a go operating signals and changing lines.

There are trains dotted all about to look at. An archaic industrial engine gives rides, or you can have a go on one of two narrow-gauge trains which negotiate short tracks from a miniature station (50p per person on weekdays). There's lots of information around and the volunteers running the place are more than willing to talk about the exhibits and railway matters in general. Their efforts are often disrupted by events beyond their control so ring first to check what's going on.

> "This is one for real train buffs as you can have a go operating signals and changing lines"

There are gigantic games mapped out on the ground outside Children's Corner and adults can plonk themselves on a bench whilst the young'uns play noughts and crosses, draughts or target practice. Inside we met Harry, a local artist whose work is on display. He chalked an engine on a board and invited our kids to colour it in. Giant jigsaws, made by Harry, can be completed, and there are some enormous dominoes to shuffle around.

Further in you can climb into the cab of a Class 47 Diesel to see its controls or you may prefer peeping out of the 1845 Columbine. There's an expansive model railway and the kids can have a go at operating it – the signal box will keep aspiring Fat Controllers busy for some time directing the trains. As we went to have a go at the block system we heard a Cheshire burr declare "My farvur wurrked on the railway" and there behind the door was a dummy dressed up as the signal man. Go on into the Lever Room that looked to me like the inside of a television set, and which despite its complex array of wires, lights, buzzers and bells, is a simplified version of the original.

The cafe is built around an exposed railway arch and has old photographs and pictures lining the walls to bring you more railway history. We sat on a well-padded old waiting room bench next to a 1d ticket machine, and tucked into the home-made barm cakes sold there. As the cafe is not open all the time, you can sit here to eat your own picnic or use the Safeway cafe opposite.

Upstairs (you'll have to either leave the buggy below or heave it up the steps) is the Control Room and Viewing Balcony. From up here you can hear the tannoy and look down at the tracks on either side to see the present day trains that run in and out of Crewe station. The Control Room gives you more levers to work and there's someone to supervise you as you guide your trains from A to B with a plan above illuminating your train's journey. There is more information on the walls, including a list of railway terminology. Did you know that if you disagree with someone's proposal your reply would be "Slattern"? There's many more like that and we imagined the conversations to be had using just one-worded phrases.

You'll find that the shop has plenty of locomotive type things to buy. We found a guard's hat for £1.50 and there is a selection of things for under £1.00. As one child suggested eating his ice-cream in the car, I was able to put my new-found knowledge to use with "Slattern", of course, being the reply.

Fact File

- ADDRESS: Railway Age, Crewe Heritage Centre, Vernon Way, Crewe, Cheshire
- TELEPHONE: 01270 212130
- DIRECTIONS: Junctions 16 or 17 off M6, head for Crewe and follow the brown signs
- PUBLIC TRANSPORT: Crewe Station is a few minutes walk
- DISTANCE: 45 miles
- TRAVEL TIME: 1 hour
- OPENING: Daily 10.00am-4.00pm, February to October
- PRICES: Weekdays £2.50 adults, £1.50 children, under-3's free. Weekends £3.50/£2.00 or £10.00 family
- RESTAURANT FACILITIES: Limited opening
- NAPPY CHANGING FACILITIES: Yes
- HIGH CHAIRS: No
- DOGS: Yes
- PUSHCHAIR-FRIENDLY: Yes
- NEARBY: Nantwich with historical buildings, shops and eating places. Queens Park has boating, putting, crazy golf

Croxteth Hall & Country Park

You'll get real value for effort when you travel through the streets of Liverpool to find the old home of Lord Sefton with its Hall, gardens and rare breeds farm. Now run by Liverpool City Council, the estate has been made into a family-friendly complex, complete with models of its former inhabitants that really bring Croxteth Hall to life.

We went into the Hall accompanied by loud exclamations of "wow" with comparisons made to the home of the film character Richie Rich. A wide red-carpeted staircase invites you to tiptoe up in search of that missing glass slipper, whilst the servants' quarters bring you back to earth. Our children were enthralled by the mannequins going about their humble business within the kitchens: one enquired why if the Pastry Maid had lived here for hundreds of years, she wasn't a skeleton by now!

Upstairs we had a peek at the more opulent side of life when an attendant helped me to lift the buggy up the grand staircase to where Lord and Lady Sefton were to be found relaxing in their various rooms. Whenever I entered one of the rooms I had to suppress the impulse to apologise to the grand figures for the intrusion I had made, but apart from this embarrassment we were all enchanted by the Hall's silent inhabitants and re-created room settings. There is lots to find out as notice-boards explain each scene and the duties or customs depicted.

Near the Hall is a Victorian walled garden with ornate fruit trees, bee hives and vegetable patches just like those that were tended for the gentry. I was reminded of

> **"A wide red-carpeted staircase invites you to tiptoe up in search of that missing glass slipper"**

☞ "The Secret Garden" as we walked between flower beds and along the glass houses. The surrounding high walls reminded the kids of our terraced back yard at home and I received lots of suggestions as to how we could turn our bit of turf into something as splendid as this.

Pathways through the grounds are well-maintained for buggy manoeuvres and there is a games field set aside for families to enjoy their frisbee or football games away from those pursuing more sedate activities. Picnic benches are dotted about and you can choose from many shady trees to flop beneath. Our trekking round the grounds was interrupted in favour of a bit of rough and tumble in the adventure playground. This is for the under-12's only and is constructed of wood.

Nearby is the farm, stuffed full of rare breeds and curious looking beasts; for example the six-horned sheep that rather concerned our children, until one of them admitted that having so much fighting equipment could be quite useful! There are pigs of different shapes, sizes, patterns and colours, and cattle with a variety of histories. The animals all have notices informing you of what area of Britain each one was popular in and in which century.

We ate our lunch in an education room within the cow shed. As beef paste sandwiches were consumed we were serenaded by a chorus of bellows and trumpets, making us rather nervous of venturing out to meet the cattle. Once the ice was broken, though, we were brave enough to stand next to the enormous head of a bull as he enjoyed a cool hose down.

En route back to the car we passed the miniature railway, a privately-run venture which only costs 30p a circuit, so the kids went round twice, bringing a joyful end to a fascinating day.

Fact File

- ADDRESS: Croxteth Hall and Country Park, Liverpool, Merseyside
- TELEPHONE: 0151 228 5311
- DIRECTIONS: M57, junction 4, follow brown signs on A580
- PUBLIC TRANSPORT: Buses from Liverpool City Centre
- DISTANCE: 40 miles
- TRAVEL TIME: 1 hour
- OPENING: Daily 11.00am-5.00pm from April to September. Farm all year 11.00am-4.00pm in winter
- PRICES: All-inclusive ticket £3.50 adults, £1.75 children, £8.80 family, under-3's free. Separate admissions available
- RESTAURANT FACILITIES: Yes
- NAPPY CHANGING FACILITIES: Yes
- HIGH CHAIRS: Yes
- DOGS: No
- PUSHCHAIR-FRIENDLY: Yes
- NEARBY: Liverpool City Centre houses a number of museums and art galleries

Haddon Hall

IF YOUR KIDS LIKE MYSTERIOUS-LOOKING CASTLES THEY WILL FIND Haddon Hall a treat. It's got all the trappings of a legendary kingdom with a long driveway commencing from great gates, through a stone arch, taking you over the moat bridge and up the hill to the Duke of Rutland's domain. There's a restaurant, pleasant gardens, museum and the Hall itself to explore, which includes the original medieval kitchen.

It is a beautiful drive through the countryside to Bakewell. Once we left the motorway to cruise through Cheshire I felt as though we were in Postman Pat country. There are fields galore with farm houses and animals peppering the scenery and stone-built villages pass by within a blink of an eye. Gradually these become fewer as you climb towards the hilly roads of the Peak District. We stopped in Buxton for lunch and a stretch before going on towards Bakewell, finally coming across the brown signs that directed us to Haddon Hall.

You park (50p) on the opposite side of quite a busy road. A souvenir shop is nestled beneath the arch next to the ornate entrance gates and from here the driveway takes you up towards the Hall past the restaurant and toilets to the summit.

"Medieval kitchens of wood and stone date back 600 years"

You'll need to leave your buggy, if you have one, in the courtyard. As we were doing this the boys became engrossed in the nearby Museum – they were particularly interested in a shoe which had been found when the nursery was excavated, dated from the 17th century. There were lots of other bits and bobs to be seen that were found during the early 1900's when the hall was re-opened, all accompanied by interesting information.

The chapel is also through the courtyard and has an effigy of a little boy who would have inherited the title had he not died. Services are still held here so it is a quiet and peaceful place. Our ever-curious eldest found a tiny padlocked door in a recess outside. He peeped through the cracks in the ancient oak to see a tunnel and whooped with excitement at this secret passage. At the other side of the courtyard a stone spiral staircase takes you up to a couple of tiny bedrooms.

When we eventually got into the main part of the Hall I marvelled at the intricate beams on the ceiling until I was dragged away by a small person who had found another staircase. At the top, tapestries and paintings cover the walls but again I wasn't able to pore over them for long, as our impatient guide had got wind of the medieval kitchens and hurried us on. These rooms of wood and stone date back 600 years. You will see the original 14th century work-tops, worn through in places, and the block where carcasses were chopped and perhaps also slaughtered. A great oak box that once held brine, and recesses where bread was baked are all here, just as they have been through the centuries. Look out for scorch marks left on the beamed ceiling by homemade tallow candles.

We found an early telephone that the 9th Duke of Rutland installed when he re-opened the Hall after a long period of dormancy. He decided to leave these kitchens intact with their antiquities and so had new ones installed where the restaurant now stands. (The telephone was there for him to order his meals which would have been sent through a tunnel). These efforts have done our heritage a great service and a roam around Haddon Hall is quite an eye-opener.

The gardens can be reached via the Hall only and are a treat for lovers of flowers, being ornate and formal with pathways here and there. We sat in the summer house and enjoyed the view, although our two scallywags explored a bit and found a path that leads right round to the front of the Hall. From this high position the counties of Derbyshire and Cheshire can be enjoyed as their hills and farmland stretch far beyond, not to mention the long and windy road back home.

Fact File

- ADDRESS: Haddon Hall, Bakewell, Derbyshire
- TELEPHONE: 01629 812855
- DIRECTIONS: A6 via Chapel-en-le-Frith and Buxton, to Bakewell. Signposted from there
- PUBLIC TRANSPORT: Buses from Buxton (15 miles) stop outside the Hall. Nearest train station is Matlock or Chesterfield
- DISTANCE: 50 miles
- TRAVEL TIME: 1 hour 30 minutes
- OPENING: Daily 11.00am-5.00pm from 1 April to 30 September
- PRICES: Adults £5.50, children £3.00, family £14.75 and under-5's free
- RESTAURANT FACILITIES: Yes
- NAPPY CHANGING FACILITIES: Yes
- HIGH CHAIRS: One
- DOGS: No
- PUSHCHAIR-FRIENDLY: No
- NEARBY: Buxton Caves in Buxton

Peckforton Castle

THIS IS A MOST MYSTERIOUS-LOOKING CASTLE, REACHED BEHIND great gates and up a sinuous drive between the trees. Hidden away in the woodlands with a great sandstone drawbridge across its moat, the castle looks just the place to find a band of highway men attacking an evil king or perhaps even a Victorian gentleman on the trail of a crime.

Parking is nearby, in a clearing. You enter the castle by way of the drawbridge and go through immense doors which are set in a stone arch. Via the cafe you arrive in the courtyard, where the Chapel, castle walls and battlements enclose you in their magical setting.

Our footsteps echoed as we followed the tour around the castle. As you enter each area you are confronted by a talking mannequin who tells the tale of where you are. Each is suitably dressed, so be prepared to meet a jester, a grand gentleman and a headless figure to name but a few. Although they can be a bit ghostly, it is a wonderful way to bring the castle and its history to life. Each of your 'guides' directs you on to the next room as he finishes, but there's no

"Wrap yourself in tales and legends with its battlements, ghostly guides and cellar"

problem with timing, as, if you want to linger, you can just hang on longer, and after a pause, he'll just go through the whole lot again!

We proceeded round at our own pace in this vein, starting with the Chapel, where a gentleman of the cloth received us and conjured up the worship that has passed through the centuries. Then it was on to the Great Hall, Drawing and Dining Rooms, Long Gallery and Ghost Gallery.

There was an air of informality about the place when we went round as the staff were busying themselves for a wedding reception that night. This left the antics of our lot unnoticed, so there was no hushing or embarrassed restraining of squirming limbs to avoid censure by museum staff.

The castle is privately owned and has lots of rooms and corridors to explore. It has been used by a couple of film companies of late and the scenery erected is left to enhance the whole experience for adventure-hungry visitors like us. I could almost imagine Robin Hood swinging round the Hall from the balconies that 20th Century Fox erected a few years ago. On a more sinister note are the prisons in the cellar where Sherlock Holmes (Jeremy Brett) sleuthed through the passages, in search of clues. Photographs are hung along the walls with information about these productions, as well as the history of the castle.

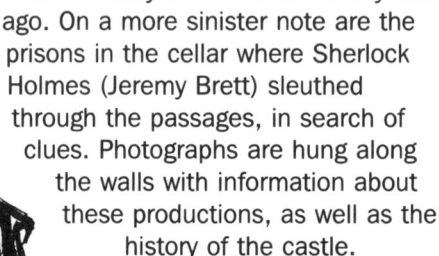

We went up some spiral steps, out onto the battlements to gaze over the beautiful scenery. For 20p you can spy through a telescope and survey the Cheshire fields, villages and roads. This was quite a treat for my little Princes as they strutted up and down and peered through the telescope at their fiefdom.

The woodlands in which the castle stands are full of plants and small rustling animals, and you can explore or play hide and seek. There's a bar and toilets in the old stable block, where you can sit in the horses' stalls to drink, or picnic in the courtyard. We had an ice cream on one of the benches that sit out here and were joined rather suddenly by a motley collection of hens and cats. Our four-year-old ended up on the wooden table itself, demanding that someone call off the chortling ginger fowl that was after his lolly. The tea shop is back at the entrance.

Peckforton is a good place to visit in bad weather as the sights and exhibits are all indoors. You could combine it with some of the other castles in the area, or stay here and simply wrap yourself in the tales and legends of Peckforton with its battlements, ghostly guides and cellar. Summer Sundays are a good bet for really getting into the atmosphere, as medieval scenes are re-enacted on the green.

Fact File

- ADDRESS: Peckforton Castle, Tarporley, Cheshire
- TELEPHONE: 01829 260930
- DIRECTIONS: M56 junction 10, and take the A49 in direction of Tarporley and Whitchurch. Turn right at Spurstow to Peckforton
- PUBLIC TRANSPORT: None
- DISTANCE: 40 miles
- TRAVEL TIME: 1 hour
- OPENING: Daily 10.00am-6.00pm 10 April to 13 September
- PRICES: Adults £2.50, children £1.50, under-5's free
- RESTAURANT FACILITIES: Yes
- NAPPY CHANGING FACILITIES: No
- HIGH CHAIRS: No
- DOGS: No
- PUSHCHAIR-FRIENDLY: Yes, some stairs
- NEARBY: Nantwich with its museum and historical church and other buildings. Cheshire Herbs, a specialist herb nursery, is near Tarporley (on A49, just beyond A54 junction)

Speke Hall

Some remnants of history which have casually escaped the shipwrecks of time . . .

THIS BLACK–AND–WHITE–TIMBERED HOUSE NESTLES BETWEEN LAWNS of rich green grass and woodlands, kept safe from late 20th century city life by the National Trust. Like a giant liquorice allsort it perches triumphantly on the edge of a Liverpool industrial estate near the city's airport. Planes soar noisily above its wooden beams and landscaped-gardens but you can walk serenely in its green and pleasant land or scamper with the kids through the clough and water garden. The Tudor Hall itself has secrets to discover within although it's not advisable with toddlers who like to handle things.

We entered the dimly-lit building (blinds are drawn to preserve the furnishings) via a tiny opening in the great wooden door. Buggies must be left in the foyer and plastic slippers are provided for stiletto-wearers. Front carrying baby slings only are permitted, so no back packs either. There's a reverent atmosphere and touching is not welcomed – if you're carrying a baby around control may be difficult. Because the house passed directly into the hands of the National Trust everything is as it was after the Watt family restored it during the 1800s and enthusiastic children like ours may have to be stopped from wrecking the joint! Having said that, there is a specially produced Children's Guidebook available for a small extra charge (£1.40), and older children would probably enjoy their visit if they went round with that. You may decide to restrict the family's day out to enjoying the exquisite

> "The rooms show the plush surroundings of the gentry in bygone times"

exterior of Speke Hall from the grounds, but I was pleasantly surprised by my seven-year-old's response to the interior: "Mum, you said it wouldn't be very childish but it's excellent".

The rooms show the plush surroundings of the gentry in bygone times and there are unpaid stewards in each one who answer questions with a genuine air of affection. You can peer into the loo and the Priest's Look Out. The time when Catholics were persecuted by the Crown is conjured up with a glance at the room in which the priest hid and at the peep hole provided to warn him of danger. His ladder is still there, leading to sanctuary in the roof.

The floor boards creek as visitors traipse through the corridors, sniffing the highly polished old oak and marvelling at the aesthetic architectural treasures. Another awe-inspiring exhibit is the spacious kitchen. You can walk around this room and marvel at the old utensils and cleverly placed props.

Outside enjoy the rose garden and discover the rear of the building by peeping through gaps in the bordering hedges. There is a tea shop with decor in keeping with the historic elegance of its surroundings and toilets with baby changing facilities. Once we'd meandered along the pathways and investigated the tall trees of the clough we made our way back to the car and headed to a more modern setting for tea.

The original Liverpool airport was just next door to the Hall and a long bank of earth was built to protect the building from environmental damage. If you climb to the top of the bank you can see for miles with the hills of Wales and landmarks of Liverpool coming into view.

You now have to go down the road to the airport but the aeroplanes still zoom low over the historic site. We settled ourselves in the restaurant next to one of the big windows overlooking a runway and watched small bi-planes coming and going and a fuel tanker doing its stuff. There was a little fire engine busying round and various groups of people came under the scrutiny of our binoculars. It's amazing to think that Speke Hall has such a 20th century neighbour. The past inhabitants of its rooms may once have mused upon flying machines and it prompted me to wonder what might happen next door to our house in a few hundred years!

Fact File

- ADDRESS: Speke Hall, The Walk, Liverpool
- TELEPHONE: 0151 427 7231
- DIRECTIONS: Follow signs to Liverpool Airport from junction 4 of M62, or junction 12 of M56
- PUBLIC TRANSPORT: Bus and 30-minute walk
- DISTANCE: 25 miles
- TRAVEL TIME: 30 minutes
- OPENING: Tuesday-Sunday (and Bank Holiday Mondays) 4 April to end of October 1.00pm-5.30pm. Weekends only November to 13th December
- PRICES: Adults £4.00, children £2.00, under-5's free. Family £10.00. Grounds only £1.40 adults and 70p children. Free to National Trust members
- RESTAURANT FACILITIES: Yes
- NAPPY CHANGING FACILITIES: Yes
- HIGH CHAIRS: Yes
- DOGS: No
- PUSHCHAIR-FRIENDLY: Outside only

Wigan Pier

FOR A THEATRE TRIP WITH A DIFFERENCE HEAD HERE. DECLARED AS the world's most famous pier, it sits by the Leeds-Liverpool canal within the centre of Wigan. It houses a museum depicting the lives of folk who lived in Wigan at the turn of the century and is home to a resident Theatre Company. Throughout the day they enact the daily trials and tribulations that typically befell the working class people and you'll find that you're not so much an audience as a member of the crowd at a demo or perhaps a disgraced school child hauled in front of the class. In addition there's a re-created Victorian town to wander round, a water bus and the world's largest original working mill steam engine. You can also do some lovely waterside walks.

At the entrance the scene is set as holiday time, a train at the station with Blackpool beckoning from the other side of the foyer. From here go on through the dark narrow tunnels of a coal mine, where shovels scrape and where we passed a miner extracting coal for his pony to haul.

> **"Be a Time Lord and talk to the Wiganers with their clogs and shared privy"**

Next, we sat in the market square outside Kellett's Dispensing Chemist where an 'argument' ensued. Things got a bit heated and the lady next to me was asked to brandish a Votes For Women placard whilst I suddenly became "Agnes wi' thi' babbie t'feed". The "babbie" was incongruously nestled in a 1990's buggy and was watching the proceedings with interest.

On the next floor there's a 1900's pub complete with barmaid. You can sit and listen to the rumble of men's talk within the lounge before going on to make more discoveries. The Boer War and its effect on the local community is poignantly depicted with true testimonies and memorabilia. There is a collier's cottage where under garments can be viewed on the washing line in the yard and living conditions within the back-to-backs vividly described by anecdotes. After visiting so many grand homes it was refreshing to peek into the lives of more ordinary folk!

Later the Victorian characters swept through the museum with a 50-minute play and the audience in tow. You'll find you may often be an unwitting accomplice. Throughout the play children stood or sat transfixed and even our four-year-old didn't lose interest. We were amazed how the actors were able to pick details from the audience which they skilfully improvised into the act.

Don't miss the School Room. You have to line up in single file, boys one side and girls the other. When the school mistress arrives any boy wearing a hat will have it removed, whilst giggling or talking will receive a severe reprimand. Sensitive souls will need to be prepared for this experience especially if they are just about to start school! The stern Miss Catchpole put us through our times tables and we were ordered to get slates out of our desks and write our names. I was labelled a Jezebel for wearing jewellery in class. After a rendition of "All Things Bright and Beautiful" and swearing allegiance to Queen Victoria we filed past for a lice inspection and back into the present day. Phew!

In need of a bit of relaxation we headed out onto the quay and waited for the water bus to arrive. Buggies need to be carried up and down steps here and babies have to sit on a lap but the skippers are very helpful. It's a leisurely journey over to the Mill and you can come and go between the two all day. If you fancy going further afield, on summer Sundays longer boat trips down the canal can be taken three times a day for a small additional charge.

At the Mill you can browse round the machinery room and see the steam engine and cotton-making demonstrations. The Pantry over there is a large cafe with its own exhibits, including an enormous mixer. After lunch we found the Trencherfield Gardens with waterside weeping willows and small play area that has some great stuff for disabled kids. Hopping back on the water bus we explored round the town again, taking in the cloggers, bolt makers, textile workers, tinsmiths, basket weavers and foundry workers. There are even Victorian peep show machines along the promenade, a magic lantern show and a signal box where, of course, George Formby can be heard. You'll get a good sing-song in the Music Hall too, with its clairvoyant show and yet more audience participation. Again, the kids loved it.

If you want to be a Time Lord and talk to the Wiganers with their clogs and shared privy then you'll have a great day here. One important piece of advice though – don't be late for Miss Catchpole's lesson!

Fact File

- ADDRESS: Wigan Pier, Wallgate, Wigan, Greater Manchester
- TELEPHONE: 01942 323666/244888 (recorded)
- DIRECTIONS: Signposted from M6 junction 26 or M61, junction 6. On the A49, 2 minutes from town centre
- PUBLIC TRANSPORT: Wigan Station is 10-minute walk
- DISTANCE: 20 miles
- TRAVEL TIME: 30 minutes
- OPENING: 10.00am-5.00pm Monday to Thursday, 11.00am-5.00pm weekends and Good Friday
- PRICES: Adults £5.10, children £4.10, family £14.50, under-5's free. Reduced prices in the winter
- RESTAURANT FACILITIES: Yes
- NAPPY CHANGING FACILITIES: Yes
- HIGH CHAIRS: Yes
- DOGS: No
- PUSHCHAIR-FRIENDLY: Yes
- NEARBY: Haigh Country Park (01942 832895)

Up, Down, There & Back

East Lancashire Railway

And she blew . . .whooh ooh!

LIKE OTHER RETIREMENT HOMES FOR OLD ENGINES, THIS ONE IN BURY is staffed by volunteers. However, a partnership with local authorities has enabled the line to provide good facilities for families without losing any of its historic feel. Thus, you can get a wheelchair or two easily on board, with plenty of room for your double buggies and pushchairs, not to mention the kitchen sink (that's what it always feels like when *we* go anywhere). Everyone, therefore, can come and travel on a steam train in comfort, through the picturesque countryside between Bury and Rawtenstall, perhaps hopping off en route to visit other historic or interesting places.

> "The Station Master and Porter bustle about in peak caps and smart uniforms"

Follow the signs through Bury town centre to the East Lancashire Railway Station, then, with this on your left, carry on to a car park. Free on Sundays, this is a two-minute walk from the station, where you'll find yourself in a foyer which doubles as ticket office and souvenir shop. Here sits an old clock and luggage scales, whilst the Station Master and Porter bustle about in peak caps and smart uniforms. There is plenty of seating and old signs surround the walls. If you bring a grandparent along they'll delight at the 50s/60s feel, while youngsters will marvel at the Thomas paraphernalia.

The carriages are highly polished and plush, with a choice of classes to choose from. We did the straight run up the line: a remarkably lazy way to spend a Sunday afternoon. Done like this, the round trip takes a little under two hours. Perhaps next time we'll venture out at Heywood to call on Chamber House Urban Farm, or call in at the mills where *Brass* was filmed at Summerseat and the train passes over a picturesque viaduct.

There's lots to do and see at Ramsbottom too. Get off here for a closer look at Peel Tower. There's also a Cat museum, Heritage Centre and park. Irwell Vale is a good spot for a ramble or you could continue to Rawtenstall to find its museum, park, Groundwork Countryside Centre or the 18th Century Weaver's Cottage.

Simply riding on the trains, however, is a treat in itself. What with the chuffing and chugging, whistling and tooting, the age of steam seems magical and exciting. You can watch the engine being filled with water, stand next to its enormous wheels and pistons, smell the smoke and soot and absorb the railway jargon and announcements.

Once on board the heat will creep up little toes, legs and tummies, to warm up cold noses. Scarves and hats can slide to the floor as frosty fields glide by. The tunnels were terribly exciting, especially before the lights went on in the train! We spotted a farmer rounding up his flock with the help of his dog, a field of sheep who were accompanied by a llama and curious looking industrial buildings, probably from years past. The scenery is breathtaking with hills, bridges, fields and monuments and you get to see a good cross section of Lancashire's architectural and agricultural history.

We were offered post cards, depicting the very engine that pulled us, for 20p and people regularly came round to collect our rubbish. There are baby changing facilities on board, whilst our elder two made umpteen trips to the loo, as it was something of a novelty. There's an inspirational carriage for parties with wheelchairs too.

Sleepily, we eventually rumbled back into Bury, having been lulled by the swaying motion and warmth. A replica of the old Tram Depot, made up of some of its original bricks, stands on Platform 2 and houses toilets, baby changing and restaurant facilities. Its green and cream colour scheme and elegantly arched windows merge perfectly with the older architecture, confirming that those staid Victorians knew what they were doing when it came to design. The cafe provides a great vantage point for watching the huffing and puffing or hissing and clanking over on Platform 4.

Fact File

- ADDRESS: Bolton Street Station, Bury, Lancashire
- TELEPHONE: 0161 764 7790
- DIRECTIONS: M66 junction 4, into Bury and follow signs in centre
- PUBLIC TRANSPORT: Metrolink trains to Bury from Altrincham and Manchester, short walk from station to railway
- DISTANCE: 15 miles
- TRAVEL TIME: 30 minutes
- OPENING: Weekends and Bank Holidays all year. Wednesday-Sunday in summer school holidays
- PRICES: Adult return £6.00, children £4.00, under-3's free
- RESTAURANT FACILITIES: Yes
- NAPPY CHANGING FACILITIES: Yes
- HIGH CHAIRS: Yes
- DOGS: Yes
- PUSHCHAIR-FRIENDLY: Yes
- NEARBY: Bury museums, craft centre and bird sanctuary

Keighley & Worth Valley Railway

THIS PRESERVED STEAM RAILWAY RUNS BETWEEN KEIGHLEY STATION and Oxenhope via four villages. It takes about 80 minutes to do the round trip along the 5-mile stretch or you can get off at any station and hop back on again. As someone who first climbed aboard with the Maghull 4th pack of Brownies, I can say that it is a memorable trip to make. Some services have a buffet car and there are facilities at each station as well as gift shops. In the winter, when the stations are lit by Britain's third largest line of gas lamps, an early evening trip is magical.

We started our journey by steam at Oxenhope where there's a museum, picnic area, free parking, and you get a good view of the engines and hustle and bustle of a 1950's station. The small museum is free and it takes about 20 minutes to look round the old trains. After lifting the children up to see the driver with his controls, coal and glowing fire we clambered aboard a coach to enjoy the bouncy curves of its antique seating.

"Puffs of steam rose from behind a bend as the great black beast chuffed towards us"

Haworth is the first stop, followed by Oakworth, where The Railway Children was filmed. We got off here for a look round. It looks just the same as it did in the film: I had to explain to my seven-year-old why Perks was absent but there were plenty of other uniformed officials to open and close the gate, polish the gas lights and poke the waiting room fires. A couple of barrows holding trunks and milk churns stand as though left behind by Perks and the white letters on the grass bank spelling Oakworth are still here.

The family sat in the waiting room enjoying the crackling log fire whilst I meandered along the platform. It was a misty October day and the fog reminded me of the scene in the film where Roberta's father appears from out of the engine's steam and into her arms. The booking office, like everything else, has been preserved just as it was when it was declared obsolete for general commuting in the 1950's. There is a portrait of Queen Victoria, that monarch of the age of steam, old telephones, another log fire and other bits and pieces. A tall, thin ticket machine still dispenses platform tickets so you can visit without the train ride for 20p if you just want to pop in.

We knew our train was imminent when a bell sounded and someone bustled out, Perks-fashion, to open the white gate. We craned our necks to see along the snake of track, the whoooing of an engine declaring it near, and stared until puffs of steam rose from behind a bend as the great black beast chuffed towards us. Once it had hissed and creaked to a stop, windows were pulled down and hands stretched over to fumble for the door handles before families emerged.

If you want to get out at the next station, Damems, you need to tell the guard. As Britain's smallest station, it doesn't warrant an automatic stop so the train sails by on most journeys. Chugging through the Yorkshire countryside there's lots to see and even the baby gazed out of the window. Our son pointed out a small humped back bridge, stating that a Troll probably lived underneath and I could well believe it!

A long tunnel marks the approach to Ingrow (West) Station and if windows are open the white steam rolls into the carriage. Here there is a Vintage Carriage Museum (small entrance fee) with old coaches and audio presentations. The experiences of the ordinary folk who used the railway and the plush carriages provided for the more wealthy Victorians are vividly brought to life, whilst travelling through London during the Blitz is portrayed as a very scary business.

Keighley, at the end of the line, is the largest station and you could start from here if you prefer. We hopped out to get sandwiches and coffee from the buffet on the platform and to watch the huffing and puffing engine being uncoupled, driven under a bridge in clouds of steam, changing direction on the working turntable and chuffing importantly back to the carriages waiting for the return journey to Oxenhope.

If you're planning to spend the day here the Family Rover ticket allows limitless hopping on and off to inspect the stations and take advantage of the buffet services or picnic areas provided. You could combine your trip with an excursion into Haworth for its Bronteana and delightful shops (there's a bus stop opposite the station). The Parsonage Museum and Parish Church are well worth a browse and can be found at the top of the cobbled Main Street.

Fact File

- ADDRESS: The Railway Station, Haworth, Keighley, West Yorkshire
- TELEPHONE: 01535 645214/647777 (talking timetable)
- DIRECTIONS: M62 junction 21, via Smithy Bridge to Littleborough and Hebden Bridge. A6033 on to Oxenhope and Keighley
- PUBLIC TRANSPORT: Train and W.Yorkshire metro to Keighley via Leeds. 5-minute walk from Keighley station
- DISTANCE: 35 miles
- TRAVEL TIME: 1 hour
- OPENING: Weekends and Bank Holidays all year, midweek during spring and summer school holidays
- PRICES: Return £5.20 adult, £2.60 children, £13.00 family, under-5's free. Day Rover for unlimited travel £6.50 adult, £3.25 children, £15.00 family
- RESTAURANT FACILITIES: Yes
- NAPPY CHANGING FACILITIES: No
- HIGH CHAIRS: No
- DOGS: Yes
- PUSHCHAIR-FRIENDLY: Yes
- NEARBY: Bronte Parsonage Museum (01535 642323), or the beautiful scenery of Bronte Country, Skipton, The Pennines and Yorkshire Dales

Llangollen Wharf & Steam Railway

All was a-shake and a-shiver, glints and gleams and sparkles, rustle and swirl, chatter and bubbles

Forget the traffic jams as the busy A5 enters the Welsh Mountains, and make a trip to Llangollen itself for an opportunity to step back in time, and see how people coped with getting out and about a century ago. With its horse-drawn canal boat rides and steam railway Llangollen is a treat for transport freaks, plus a charming and bustling small town.

Make your way down to the river as you arrive in the town. You'll see the train station next to Castle Street Bridge, and the canal boat rides operate from the wharf above the station. Look out for the blackboards down by the bridge giving times of the boats running that day. To get up to the canal is a fairly steep short climb by steps or ramped pathway, or you can access it by road. Once up there you are straight onto the towpath with toddlers needing watching by the open canal.

> **"With its open sides and covered roof the old-fashioned narrow boat is ideal if it is rainy"**

We were lucky, hopping immediately onto a boat, pushchair and all. There was plenty of room, and the kids stood on the bench seats spotting the huge perch and roach streaming past. Other thrills were meeting another boat coming the other way (yes, there is room), the tunnel, and the fishermen on the towpath who caught an enormous fish just as we passed.

The horse pulls you along under the trees at slow walking pace through stunning upland scenery to Berwyn and back. The entire return trip lasts 45 minutes – just the right length to maintain interest. With its open sides and covered roof the old-fashioned narrow boat is ideal if it is rainy, but mind you dry your seat first.

Horse-drawn canal trips run frequently throughout the day. If you just miss one, spend the waiting time making friends with the horses kept in small stable boxes alongside the Centre. Alternatively, try the cakes on offer in the tearoom, and admire the view over the town from the outside terrace, or try the licensed restaurant.

Real enthusiasts may want to try the 2-hour trip from the Wharf to Pont Cysyllte aquaduct on the Thomas Telford narrow boat. Fantastic views, a castle to admire from afar, and the dizzying 126' high aquaduct are on offer, but phone in advance to book at busy periods.

From May to September steam trains run hourly from the Victorian station below the Wharf, but check times in advance. The return trip up to Carrog takes about 1 hour 20 minutes. The train steams up into the mountains in restored carriages, giving a real taste of what life was like in 'the old days'. After stopping at Berwyn with great views of the river Dee rushing below there is a long pull through a very dark tunnel.

We got out at the beautiful 1950's station at Carrog and inspected the engine. Although described as medium-sized by the driver it looked enormous to us: all shining black coachwork, gleaming trim and enough hisses, puffs and whistles to enthral any Thomas the Tank enthusiast. You can get up onto the footplate, where we were fascinated to discover that the driver actually owned the train himself (fancy trying to park that!), whilst the kids were impressed by the roaring fire and the suitably-grimy fireman, in fact a woman.

From Carrog there is a good footpath walk. Or there is a picnic spot and play area next to the platform at Glyndyfrdwy and you can get off there too and watch the comings and goings.

Back at Llangollen it is worth having a look around. It is distinctly Welsh with plenty of souvenir shops, tearooms and intriguing signposts and street names: try getting the kids to get their tongues round 'Llwybr Cyhoeddus' (public footpath)! There is a small Victorian school museum and riverbank walks and picnic spots.

Fact File

- ADDRESS: Horse Drawn Boat Centre, The Wharf, Llangollen, Clwyd. Steam Railway, The Station, Abbey Road, Llangollen, Clwyd
- TELEPHONE: 01978 860702 (canal boats), 01978 860951/860979 (railway)
- DIRECTIONS: M56/M53 to A55 and Chester, then A483 to Wrexham and on towards Oswestry. A5 into Llangollen
- PUBLIC TRANSPORT: Nearest mainline trains are 5 miles away at Ruabon. Buses from Wrexham and Ruabon hourly
- DISTANCE: 75 miles
- TRAVEL TIME: 1 hour 45 minutes
- OPENING: Canal boats daily from Easter to October 11.00am-5.00pm. Railway daily from May to October, Easter week and half-terms, and weekends rest of year
- PRICES: Boats £3.00 adults, £2.00 children, £8.00 family, under-3's free. Railway return trip £7.00 adults, £3.50 children, £17.50 family, under-4's free
- RESTAURANT FACILITIES: Yes
- NAPPY CHANGING FACILITIES: Yes
- HIGH CHAIRS: No
- DOGS: Yes
- PUSHCHAIR-FRIENDLY: Yes
- NEARBY: Dr Who exhibition, Motor Museum and Plas Newydd stately home, all in Llangollen (Tourist Information Centre 01978 860828)

Mersey Ferries

to the land that I once knew . . .

LIVERPOOL CITY CENTRE HAS LOTS OF ATTRACTIONS FOR FAMILIES, including many around the Docks, and the Wirral is also teeming with things to see and places to go. By hopping on board a ferry, though, you can visit both places in one day with a boat ride in between. The Pier Head, where the ferry leaves from, is a five-minute walk along the waterside from the Albert Dock, so we called there first. You could just as easily make your way from the Wirral side of the iver though.

At midday Fred comes out to jump onto his weather map which floats on the water in the middle of the Albert Dock arcade. You can cluster round the railings and jeer or shout "Happy Birthday Nan!" for the sound recordist to pick up, or you may prefer to continue sensibly on, in which case don't take my star-struck lot! The Tate Gallery there houses modern art and has a coffee shop and baby changing room, whilst the shopping centre itself is full of cafes, shops, more baby facilities and, of course, The Beatles Museum. Car parks are just outside and these are your best bet if you're heading for the Pier Head. On the walk down to the ferry you'll pass the Liverpool Life, Maritime and Anything to Declare Museums, all worth a visit if you've time.

> **"Sit up top and gaze at the magnificent buildings or stand at the rail and watch the surf"**

The ferry itself is just how I remember 25 years ago, except that it seemed much bigger then. Before the tunnel was built this was the main way of getting across the Mersey and, apart from the Gerry and the Pacemakers sound effects, audio tour of the sky line, and bar and cafe, is just the same as it always was. At peak travel time the shuttle service resumes to get people simply from A to B, without the touristy trappings. If you choose to cruise, however, you can sit up top and gaze at the magnificent buildings, listening to their histories, or stand at the rail and watch the surf. The kids will love having the run of the ship – watch those little ones – pointing out the lifeboats and going up and down the steps.

Hop off at Seacombe to see the aquarium (get a joint ticket with the ferry). Watch out as you enter as there's a splashing wave machine. You'll see a sign saying "Please Touch" by the babbling pool in which crabs and star fish live. Interesting facts are displayed by each exhibit and peep holes enable smaller visitors to see in at the giant lobster, conger eel and other marine life. There's a balcony from which you can look down at the pool of fish who are cleverly camouflaged against their bed. Conservation is on the agenda further along – did you know it takes 1,000,000 years for a glass bottle to degrade? Even more fascinating, my son declared, would be to know how they worked that one out. There's information about the Mersey itself with a good selection of the life forms that can be found in the estuary.

The sound of the sea and gulls and the taste of salty air all add up to a worthwhile diversion from the crossing and if motion sickness has got to you, you're only a 10-minute walk from some of the attractions on the Wirral, the Battleships at Birkenhead for instance, or you can get on one of the buses that are just outside. The number 1 will take you to New Brighton where there's a park and promenade with a stone fort reached by a causeway.

By getting back on the ferry, however, you can sail to Birkenhead and alight at the Woodside terminus to climb aboard a tram and trundle along to the old Shore Road Pumping Station or further on to Pacific Road Large Objects Museum. This is a historic journey to make as it was here, in 1860, that Europe's first tramway was established and if you want to find out more, the Visitors Centre at Woodside will fill you in or you can see aged trams and other vehicles at the Pacific Road Museum.

Your return journey on the ferry should be just the ticket for the kids and they'll be able to recognise some of the dockland places by now. As we sat up top at Woodside, deciding where to eat at The Albert Dock, a small voice cried out that the wall was moving! This prompted a lesson in optical illusions as we explained that it was we who were moving. Quite jauntily, as it happened, as the sea was a little choppy but needless to say the children loved it all the more.

You can make this trip in any weather as there are covered areas on the boat but wrap up if it's windy. Cruise tickets allow you to get on and off at each port or you can simply do the round trip and listen to the gulls, the engine, the sea, Gerry and The Pacemakers and the history of the docks.

Fact File

- ADDRESS: Mersey Ferries Ltd, Victoria Place, Wallasey, Wirral, Merseyside
- TELEPHONE: 0151 630 1030
- DIRECTIONS: Liverpool City Centre, follow signs for Pier Head
- PUBLIC TRANSPORT: Short walk from mainline and metro stations. Buses go right to Pier Head
- DISTANCE: 35 miles
- TRAVEL TIME: 45 minutes
- OPENING: Ferries daily, on the hour 10.00am-3.00pm (weekdays) or 6.00pm (weekends)
- PRICES: Adults £3.30, children £1.70, family £8.50. Under-5's free. Joint ticket with Aquarium £4.30 adults, £2.35 children, £12.30 family
- RESTAURANT FACILITIES: Cafes at termini, plenty in Albert Docks
- NAPPY CHANGING FACILITIES: Yes
- HIGH CHAIRS: Some restaurants
- DOGS: Yes
- PUSHCHAIR-FRIENDLY: Yes
- NEARBY: Art galleries and museums in Liverpool city centre

The Sun Has Got His Hat On

Freshfield Red Squirrel Reserve

. . . the squirrels filled their little sacks with nuts, and sailed away home in the evening

GRAB THE SUN SCREEN, LOOK OUT THE BUCKETS AND SPADES, LOAD the camera, root out the binoculars, and don't forget a big bag of nuts. Freshfield, just south of Southport, has rolling sand hills, an award-winning golden beach with regular tides, woodlands and red squirrels. It's just a short walk from the train station and needn't cost anything to enjoy. So for an inexpensive and varied day outdoors, make up a few sandwiches, and get out the sandals (or wellies – you can have a good time here, whatever the season).

The squirrels are protected by the National Trust, who charge a car entry fee which may seem a nuisance, but it does allow you access onto the sand, saving a bit of buggy-humping and toddler-negotiating and, depending on the time of year, you could well find an ice cream van here too.

The sand makes pushchair manoeuvres rather difficult, particularly on leaving the ramp which leads up to the beach, where you then have to shuffle down the bank. Of course it's no easier getting back up again but it's well worth the effort as the beach *is* the best one around. Older kids will love the sand hills that spread far and wide. It's a great spot for hide and seek, or tire 'em out games and if it's not warm enough to bathe on the beach itself you could have a good day out just frolicking about here and strolling through the pinewoods.

The squirrel reserve has a large colony of red squirrels (around 3,000), which is good news to conservationists. Because they don't hibernate, you'll find plenty of them to "Aaahh" over throughout the seasons and the kids will find it a treat to see so many bushy tailed imps scampering about. The extra supply of goodies that the squirrels have received from visitors has ensured their growing numbers. They will even eat from your hand and you can buy food for 30p a bag.

There's nothing artificial about it – the squirrels are completely wild and can be viewed as they run up and down trees, in and out of the scrub and as they hop from branch to branch. The scent of pine and crack of twigs beneath your feet will refresh your urban-stifled psyche. The pathways that weave through the woods are great for family walks, although you can wander off the beaten track after a squirrel, a bobbing rabbit's tail or just for fun, fun, fun. And if you don't have a family dog then borrow someone else's!

"The beach *is* the best one around"

Once you've negotiated the sand bank you'll arrive on the vast expanse of sand, part of which formed the exercise ground that the late Red Rum used. The sea does come up the beach so check on local tides before planning your trip and once you've arrived it's wise to determine which direction the tide is moving as there are no life guards. We were lucky to find a couple of pools left behind in which the kids paddled, found shells, bits of sea weed and a baby crab. They filled their buckets with the wet slop and made mud pies and sand castles galore, whilst we looked up occasionally from the nice dry ground and read the Sunday papers in peace.

There are no gimmicky, touristy things and the National Trust has sorted out toilets, complete with toddler seats and baby changing facilities. There are shops, cafes and pubs not far away, although they would entail a bit of a trek, so it's the perfect excuse for bringing a picnic. A coastal walks leaflet is available for £2.00. If you come by rail, be prepared for a squash, as it's a popular trip in the summer, or leave early.

The aroma of the pine and sea has therapeutic qualities. You can gaze at the horizon and think philosophical thoughts or, like me, you can try to fathom the best way to leave the maximum amount of sand behind, how on earth you're going to persuade your 3-year-old that it isn't a good idea to keep a dead crab for a pet, and just where IS the mountain of shells to be stored?

Fact File

- ADDRESS: Freshfield Red Squirrel Reserve, Formby, Lancashire
- TELEPHONE: 01704 878591
- DIRECTIONS: A565 to Formby, follow brown signs from Liverpool direction
- PUBLIC TRANSPORT: Train from Liverpool Central
- DISTANCE: 45 miles
- TRAVEL TIME: 1 hour
- OPENING: Daily, all year
- PRICES: Car park £2.70, free to pedestrians and National Trust members
- RESTAURANT FACILITIES: No
- NAPPY CHANGING FACILITIES: Yes
- HIGH CHAIRS: No
- DOGS: Yes
- PUSHCHAIR-FRIENDLY: In pine woods
- NEARBY: Southport town and promenade

Lytham St Annes

Oh I do like to be beside the seaside!

LYTHAM IS A SMALL COASTAL TOWN NEAR BLACKPOOL, WITH A windmill and lifeboat museum, a sandy shore-line, lake with boating, and a lovely smooth green. Next to it is the town of St Annes, with shops, cafes, promenade, Victorian pier, miniature golf and railway, and, more to the point, beach, sand hills, parkland and a Toy and Teddy Museum. Paired together, they make a quieter resort that the more glitzy Blackpool, and you can enjoy the tranquil atmosphere while still keeping the kids busy.

Starting at St Annes, and with buckets and spades at the ready, the kids will probably be keen to make a bee-line for the beach and sand dunes. It's a big sandy beach, with the sea almost disappearing from view at low tide, perfect for general larking around. Once you've got digging and burying out of the system, head for Ashton Gardens, a large park, with an impressive war memorial around which our sons cavorted, pretend guns held noisily aloft. It has prettily laid-out gardens, landscaped greens, conservatory and a gardens exhibition to enjoy, and is the best place to have a picnic if you want to avoid sandy sandwiches. There's a well-maintained play area there, handy cafe, and toilets too.

> "A landscaped promenade in front of the sands and cafes"

Go on to The Toy and Teddy Museum (01253 713705), just round the corner. It's not hard to spot, when open, as there's an enormous Rupert Bear, with a few of his more regularly-sized companions, waiting at the door. Inside you'll find six rooms full of teddies, toys and childhood memorabilia, dating back to the 1800s. There's a Fun Quiz and Teddy Trail to follow as you work your way around the house, with a lesson in social history

☞ for the young ones around every corner, whilst nostalgia suddenly jumps to the fore for us 'has-beens'. It's open 1.00pm-5.00pm daily, except Mondays and Tuesdays, in the summer and at the weekend in the winter. It costs £2.50 for adults, £1.75 children and under-3's free.

Walk back along the landscaped promenade in front of the sands and cafes, admiring the elegant facade of the pier, with a waterfall, pools and rocky cave to wander through – watch out for the drips. Have a look at the memorial in the Alpine gardens along the prom before you go, as you'll find out more about the disaster it commemorates over at the Lifeboat Museum in Lytham.

A 5-minute drive, or easy 30-minute stroll along the front (regular buses back), takes you to Lytham where there is more to see. The windmill, unmissable on the horizon with its sails still intact, is perched on the green, facing the sea. Between its curved rugged walls are fascinating exhibits, depicting important landmarks in the local history with old artefacts and mannequins to help bring them to life. You can go up to see the wheels and cogs that drove the mill, peering out at the open surroundings as you go, and think of that stalwart character of Camberwick Green (if you're as old as me). It is free to enter and is open at Easter and from Whitsun to September every day except Monday and Friday.

Alongside is the Lifeboat Museum, also free, and crammed full of marine artefacts and information. It's open Tuesdays, Thursdays and weekends from Whitsun to the end of September (closed from 1.00pm-2.00pm for lunch). We enjoyed looking at a model of the Fylde Coast, and working out where we were before heading back down to the beach again for more sandcastles.

Fact File

- ADDRESS: Tourist Information, 290 Clifton Drive South, St Annes, Lancashire
- TELEPHONE: 01253 725610
- DIRECTIONS: M61, M55, follow signs
- PUBLIC TRANSPORT: Train to St Annes from Preston
- DISTANCE: 60 miles
- TRAVEL TIME: 1 hour
- OPENING: All year
- PRICES: Free (mostly)
- RESTAURANT FACILITIES: Yes
- NAPPY CHANGING FACILITIES: No
- HIGH CHAIRS: Some restaurants
- DOGS: Yes
- PUSHCHAIR-FRIENDLY: Yes
- NEARBY: Blackpool Zoo

Morecambe Bay

Forget Mr Blobby, this is SERIOUS fun we're talking about! Just off the M6, Morecambe perches on the edge of the North West in the shadow of the historic city of Lancaster. You can lose yourselves in the commercial kaleidoscope that lines the Marine Road or melt into the sea at the sight of the Lake District hills as they frame the blue and gold shore. There's a theme park and other family entertainment, Victorian promenade splendour, play areas and shops to peruse, all jostling conveniently along a well-kept front. And with baby changing areas in some of the public loos and free paddling pools it's an ideal venue for families to spend a summer's day.

Approaching the bay from the South, after the cries of "I saw the sea first!" a shout went up in the car proclaiming the sighting of the Polo Tower. This is an enormous column, circumvented by a giant, people-carrying, 'polo mint' that glides gracefully up and down to allow panoramic views of Cumbria, the ancient sky line of Lancaster and the Yorkshire Pennines beyond. It is situated by the Frontierland Western Theme Park, which sprawls beyond a Wild West facade along the prom and has a small entrance fee.

Further along is the Happy Mount Park with lawns, flower beds,

> **"The beach offers lots of sloopy, gloopy, sandy, muddy stuff that is just EX for digging, building and excavating"**

Japanese Garden, bowling, putting, miniature golf, trampolines, Sunday Band Concerts and play area. The Park's grassy areas and benches make it ideal for sand-free picnicing. In late summer there is usually a themed exhibition here: an extravaganza of lights, illuminated fountains, animatronics and a blaze of colour bringing the peaceful setting to life. Separating the array of activities from the sea is a neat walkway, punctuated with flower beds, elegantly designed seating areas and well kept loos. There are play areas at either end and a free paddling pool.

The beach is just a couple of steps down and, when the tide's out, offers lots of sloopy, gloopy, sandy, muddy stuff that is just EX for digging, building and excavating. Or so my bucket and spade wielding pair informed me. We settled on a step, with the beckoning hills of

Wordsworth, Beatrix Potter and Wainwright on our right and had our picnic. The views are spectacular, once you put all the glitz of the other tourist attractions, quite literally, behind you, and let your mind drift out to sea.

Six miles south along the coast is the village of Heysham, with its tiny church and religious ruins. There is a nice stretch of sand here, the soft golden grainy stuff that good beaches are said to be made of. Heysham's Power Station sits incongruously amidst a nature trail, above the beach. Entrance is free to its Powerquest Visitors' Centre, where visual aids bring to life the technology of nuclear energy.

With an annual carnival, festivals and other events throughout the year, Morecambe provides ample choices for a day trip, be it from the number of more modern attractions or from the traditional sandcastle-building variety, and there'll always be something for everyone. Whether you choose to knot your hanky and roll up your trousers for an inexpensive treat or prefer simply to throw a load of loose change in your purse to investigate the laid-on entertainment, both types of attraction can be found within easy walking distance of each other.

Fact File

- ADDRESS: Tourist Information Centre, Central Promenade, Morecambe, Lancashire
- TELEPHONE: 01524 582809
- DIRECTIONS: M6, junction 33 via Lancaster
- PUBLIC TRANSPORT: Train via Lancaster
- DISTANCE: 60 miles
- TRAVEL TIME: 1 hour 30 minutes
- OPENING: Anytime
- PRICES: Free
- RESTAURANT FACILITIES: Yes
- NAPPY CHANGING FACILITIES: Yes
- HIGH CHAIRS: Some restaurants
- DOGS: Yes
- PUSHCHAIR-FRIENDLY: Yes
- NEARBY: Carnforth Steamtown (01524 732100)

Southport Promenade & Model Railway Village

AT SOUTHPORT THERE IS PLENTY TO DO WITHIN A SMALL AREA. At the Front you'll find a sandy beach, fairground, miniature railway, aquarium, lake, pitch and putt, a park, pier with a railway, and a zoo! The model railway village which opened in 1996 adds to the bonanza. Brown signs direct you to the seafront and if you're driving, there are a couple of car parks off Marine Drive which have a free bus into the shopping centre.

The sea doesn't come far in at this beach so there's plenty of flat sand for a dig. You can go up in an aeroplane on a Pleasure Flight to get a bird's eye view of the town or you might find the delights of Pleasure Land fairground itself adventurous enough. This is behind the beach and has lots of rides, big and small. Opposite is the miniature railway which takes you through Prince's Park, alongside the Marine Lake and under the Pier. Or you could opt for the larger train which, for a small charge, will carry you along the pier and back. There's even a Thomas the Tank road train which you can hop on by the Carousel. This seems to go round for ages and saves a lot of walking through King's Gardens and the park.

"The quintessential England is all laid out before your eyes"

There's a boating pool (bring your own boat) and a paddling pool in Prince's Park which are free. If you wander along the lake you can watch the Jet Skiers (or have a go yourself!) and in the summer a leisurely cruise on the Mississippi Boat or a faster ride on the Everglade Vessel will provide a good view of the islands and surrounding parkland.

In July the annual flower show fills Victoria Park and to one side is The Queen's Jubilee Nature Trail, where seaside wildlife and plants can be discovered. A short and a longer route are available, both good for kids. Nestled amid the gardens and just to the left of the pier (as you face it) you'll find a model village that's so new it's still being partly constructed. Don't let this put you off, though, as wherever there's work in progress a crew of tiny builders, complete with tools and scaffolding, have been put in place to reassure all passers-by that work will be completed soon, and, what's more, this little lot are guaranteed not to shout obscenities! It isn't just a village, but incorporates the countryside and town areas, all linked by its fully operating steam railway (the largest 45mm gauge rail in the country), a busy-looking roadway system, and a canal that winds its way through, boats and bridge included.

The quintessential England, like you'd see in *Heartbeat*, is all laid out before your eyes: neat terraces, clustered estates, two churches, a castle, windmill, cop shop and factory, providing a wonderful land of imagination, cordoned off with tall greenery from the big bad world outside, with the impressive Clifton Hotel providing a perfect backdrop. The trains chuff chuff along past a wedding party gathered for the photographer, elsewhere the farmer is tending his lambs, while the cubs and brownies are pitching their tents and a cricket match is in progress.

Great attention has been given to detail, with numerous styles of windows, doors and other architectural matters. If you have binoculars you'll see just how well it's all been crafted, on site, by hand, with obsessive detail bringing each scene to life.

There are benches dotted about so that you can sit and enjoy a picnic. Situated so close to the sea, it's likely to get breezy so come on a warm day or wrap up well. The little ones can go off and wonder at the adventures that are laid out before them while you sit and reflect on the times when the streets were free of litter. This is a land of make-believe where you might expect The Famous Five to come tearing down one of its grassy hills. Who'd blame them? It's idyllic.

Fact File

- ADDRESS: Southport Tourist Information Centre, Lord Street, Southport, Lancashire
- TELEPHONE: 01704 533333 (Tourist Information), 01704 214266 (Model Village)
- DIRECTIONS: A570 from junction 3 off the M58
- PUBLIC TRANSPORT: Train to Southport
- DISTANCE: 40 miles
- TRAVEL TIME: 45 minutes
- OPENING: Promenade, all year. Model Village mid-February-October, daily 10.00am-5.00pm
- PRICES: Promenade, free. Model Village £2.50 adults, £1.50 children, under-2's free, family £6.50
- RESTAURANT FACILITIES: Yes
- NAPPY CHANGING FACILITIES: No
- HIGH CHAIRS: No
- DOGS: Yes
- PUSHCHAIR-FRIENDLY: Yes

Notes

Other Books IN THE SERIES

ALSO AVAILABLE IN THIS SERIES:

The Heinz Guide to
DAYS OUT WITH KIDS
in the **West Country**
TRIED-AND-TESTED FUN FAMILY OUTINGS IN SOMERSET, DORSET, WILTSHIRE, AVON, GLOUCESTERSHIRE, WORCESTERSHIRE, HEREFORDSHIRE AND SOUTH WALES.
130 PAGES, PAPERBACK, £4.99

The Heinz Guide to
DAYS OUT WITH KIDS
in the **Heart of England**
TRIED-AND-TESTED FUN FAMILY OUTINGS IN WARWICKSHIRE, WORCESTERSHIRE, SHROPSHIRE, GLOUCESTERSHIRE, STAFFORDSHIRE, LEICESTERSHIRE, AND WEST MIDLANDS.
130 PAGES, PAPERBACK, £4.99

The Heinz Guide to
DAYS OUT WITH KIDS
in the **North East**
TRIED-AND-TESTED FUN FAMILY OUTINGS IN NORTHUMBERLAND, DURHAM, CLEVELAND, TYNE & WEAR AND NORTH YORKSHIRE.
138 PAGES, PAPERBACK, £4.99

The Heinz Guide to
DAYS OUT WITH KIDS
in the **South East**
TRIED-AND-TESTED FUN FAMILY OUTINGS IN KENT, SUSSEX, SURREY, HAMPSHIRE, BERKSHIRE, ESSEX, HERTFORDSHIRE, BEDFORDSHIRE AND BUCKINGHAMSHIRE.
168 PAGES, PAPERBACK, £5.99

Orders

ALL OTHER BOOKS IN THE SERIES ARE AVAILABLE FROM:
The Heinz Guide to DAYS OUT WITH KIDS
BON•BON VENTURES
24 ENDLESHAM ROAD
LONDON SW12 8JU
TEL: 0181 488 3011
FAX: 0181 265 1700

PAYMENT MAY BE MADE BY CREDIT CARD (ACCESS/VISA/MASTERCARD), OR BY CHEQUE /POSTAL ORDER PAYABLE TO BONBON VENTURES. PLEASE ALLOW £1.00 POSTAGE AND PACKING FOR THE FIRST BOOK, AND 50P PER BOOK FOR SUBSEQUENT BOOKS.

ORDER FORM

PLEASE SEND ME A COPY/IES OF HEINZ GUIDE TO DAYS OUT WITH KIDS
(TICK REQUIRED)

☐ *HEART OF ENGLAND EDITION*
   PRICE £4.99 & £1.00 POSTAGE AND PACKING
☐ *NORTH WEST EDITION*
   PRICE £4.99 & £1.00 POSTAGE AND PACKING
☐ *NORTH EAST EDITION*
   PRICE £4.99 & £1.00 POSTAGE AND PACKING
☐ *WEST COUNTRY EDITION*
   PRICE £4.99 & £1.00 POSTAGE AND PACKING
☐ *SOUTH EAST EDITION*
   PRICE £5.99 & £1.00 POSTAGE AND PACKING

I ENCLOSE MY REMITTANCE OF
£ _____

NAME _____
ADDRESS _____
_____
_____
_____

I WISH TO PAY BY CREDIT CARD
CARD NUMBER ☐☐☐☐ ☐☐☐☐ ☐☐☐☐ ☐☐☐☐
EXPIRY DATE _____ / _____
SIGNED _____

Notes

Strange But True...

Fascinating facts about the nation's favourite family brand

Heinz Only four people in the whole world know the secret blend of spices used in Heinz Baked Beans

Heinz Each day Heinz uses enough tomatoes to fill an Olympic size swimming pool

Heinz Every year Heinz uses 26,000 tonnes of vegetables, fruits and cereals, 60 million eggs, four million gallons of milk and 7,000 tons of meat

Heinz Enough cans of Heinz baby food are made to feed every British baby a can a week

Heinz Seven hundred cans of soup are made every minute

Heinz Camelford in Cornwall has its own Heinz Cream of Tomato Soup Appreciation Society. To join the club, you must take a blindfolded taste test and pick out Heinz tomato soup from the other brands